101 THINGS TO MAKE

Compiled by Janet Slingsby

Illustrated by David Mostyn

DEAN

This edition first published 1994 by
Dean, an imprint of Reed Children's Books Limited,
Michelin House, 81 Fulham Road, London SW3 6RB,
and Auckland, Melbourne, Singapore and Toronto.

ISBN 0 603 55350 8

British Library Cataloguing-in-Publication Data
A catalogue record for this book is available from the British Library

Printed in Slovenia

Contents

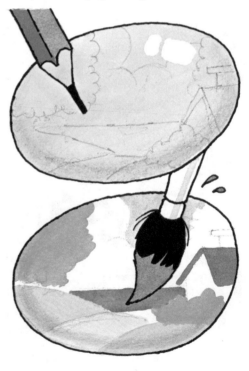

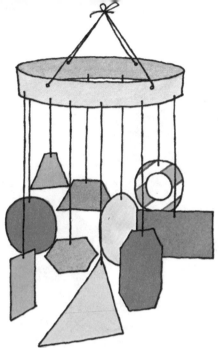

Introduction

In this book there are ideas for one hundred and one things to make – toys, games, presents, useful things, funny things and pretty things. You do not have to stop at one hundred and one. You can adapt and develop most of the ideas here to suit yourself and, I hope, by making these things you will be inspired to dream up new creations of your own.

All you need, to make most of the things in this book, are odds and ends and scraps you should be able to find around the house. Here is a list of items it is useful to save. You can keep your collection of 'useful things' in a toy box. It tells you how to make one on page 149.

Useful things to collect
All sorts of paper: plain, coloured, tissue, crepe, sweet wrappers etc.
Newspapers, old magazines and comics.
Pieces of thin card and cardboard
Cardboard boxes of all sizes
Paper bags
Scraps of material – especially felt
Leftover balls of wool
Cardboard tubes
Yoghurt pots
Plastic bottles
Tin foil
Tins with reusable lids
Egg boxes
Jam jars
Old socks and jumpers
String, cord and ribbon
Matchboxes and other small boxes
Cotton reels
Corks
Milk bottle tops
Beads and sequins
Shells and pebbles
Feathers
Pipe-cleaners

Here are a few rules that you should follow whatever you are making:
Do not make a mess.

Put newspapers down on working surfaces.

Wear old clothes or an overall.

Be very careful with glue and paint.

Do not cut anything up without asking permission first.

Clear up.

Wash out paint brushes.

Put the lids back on tubes of glue and tins of paint.

Pick up all scraps of paper etc.

Put everything away.

Toys from odds and ends

Here are some ideas for things to make from odds and ends. There are some ideas for games you can make and play with your friends, some ideas for things which will make very good presents and some ideas for toys which you can enjoy making on your own.

Woollyball

YOU WILL NEED
Thin cardboard
Wool
Darning needle
Scissors
Large glass or mug
Eggcup
Pencil

1

CUT OUT

Draw round a large glass or mug on to a piece of thin cardboard. Cut out the circle of card.

2

CUT OUT

Place an eggcup in the middle of this circle of card. Draw round the eggcup and cut that circle out of the card. You now have a ring of card.

Make a second ring exactly the same as the first.

3

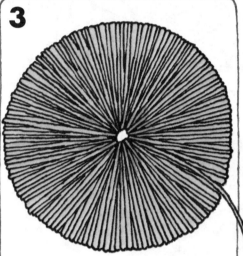

Put the two rings on top of each other and wind wool evenly around them both until the hole in the middle is nearly full. When you can't get any more wool through the hole by hand, continue winding using a darning needle.

DARNING NEEDLE

14

4

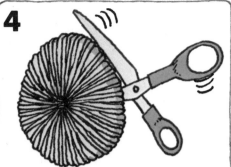

When the hole is completely full of wool, take a pair of scissors and work one blade of the scissors through the wool and into the gap between the two circles of card.

5

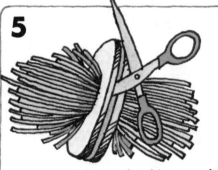

Cut through the wool making sure that one blade of the scissors stays in the gap between the two rings of card.

6

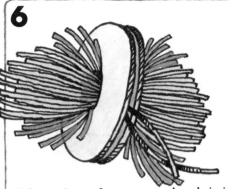

Take a piece of strong wool and tie it *very* tightly around the wool between the rings. Leave the ends of the wool long, so that you can hang up the ball. Tear the cardboard rings and pull them out.

Fluff up your woolly ball. You can use it for the top of a bobble hat or tie several small woolly balls together to make a present for a baby brother or sister.

The bigger you make the cardboard rings the bigger the woolly ball – so if you can find lots of leftover scraps of wool you can make an enormous multi-coloured ball.

Woolly mouse

1

Make a woolly ball as described on page 14. Cut out felt eyes and ears.

YOU WILL NEED
Thin cardboard
Wool
Scraps of felt
Darning needle
Scissors
Non-toxic glue suitable for sticking felt
Large glass or mug
Eggcup
Pencil

2

Stick the eyes on to the woolly ball. To secure the ears, part the wool and stick the felt well into the parting. Glue a long piece of wool on for a tail and stick some short pieces of wool under a felt nose for whiskers.

You can make other felt animals using different coloured wool and felt. Use pipe-cleaners covered with wool for legs, tails and antennae.

Woolly doll

1

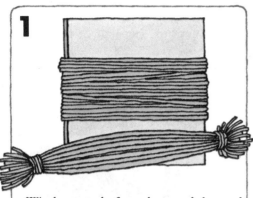

Wind a strand of wool around the card 15 times, then slide it off the card. Tie both ends with small pieces of wool to make the hands.

2

Wind some more wool around the card 30 times and slip that off. Tie wool in two places around the top to make a head. Cut the wool at the very top to make hair.

3

Put the arms through the body and tie again just beneath them.

4

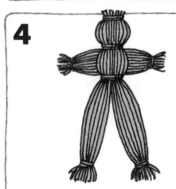

Divide the remaining wool below the arms into two and make legs and feet.

If you make a very small woolly doll you can put a safety pin through the back and wear it as a badge.

Tube snake

YOU WILL NEED
Lots of cardboard tubes
String
Your paint box, felt pens or crayons

1

Draw snakeskin patterns on all the cardboard tubes and colour them in. Paint a snake face on one tube and a snake tail on another.

3

Thread the rest of the tubes on to the string putting the face tube on last.

2

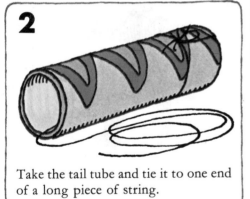

Take the tail tube and tie it to one end of a long piece of string.

18

Tube clucker

YOU WILL NEED
Cardboard tube about 9cm high
Small piece of cotton fabric
Resin (available from shops selling
    musical instruments)
Thin string
Darning needle
Sticky tape

1

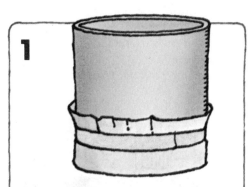

Cover one end of the cardboard tube with a piece of thin cotton fabric, fastening it very firmly with sticky tape.

2

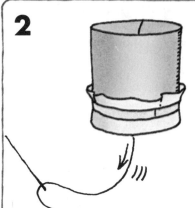

Thread a long piece of string through the needle and make a large knot in the end of the string. Put the needle down through the tube and push it out through the material so that the string is left hanging from the material. Leave about 40cm hanging.

3

Rub resin into the string and put some on your fingers. Draw your first finger and thumb down the string in short, sharp jerks. Your tube will then cluck like a chicken!

Plastic bottle skittles

1

If you want to make this game very quickly, just tape pieces of paper with different numbers on to the bottles. Then place the bottles in a triangle, stand back and roll the ball to try and knock them down. The one who gets the highest score is the winner.

2

If you've got more time it's fun to decorate the bottles and turn them into people. Cover them in paper then paint on clothes and faces.

Every time you find another empty plastic bottle you can add to your skittle collection.

Tin can stilts

YOU WILL NEED
2 old paint cans with lids and
  handles
Strong string
Scissors

1

Measure the distance from your hand to your foot when your arms are at your side.

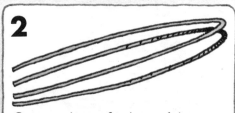

2

Cut two pieces of string each just over twice that length.

3

Tie the string to either side of the handles of each tin.

Now you can stand on the tins and walk along, using the string to move them along. Get your friends to make stilts too and you can have races. But remember you must only use these stilts outside.

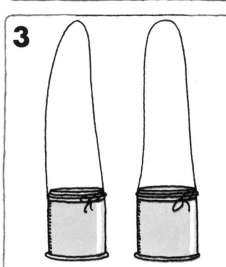

Tin can totem pole

1

TAPE

EGG
BOX

Make sure the lids are firmly on the tins, then wrap paper around each tin and fasten it with sticky tape. Now you can paint on totem pole faces. Stick on noses, beaks and ears made from cardboard – or from egg boxes.

2

Pile the tins up, putting the biggest at the bottom.

Making a tin can totem pole is extra fun if you get all your friends to bring a tin. Then each of you can decorate your own tin and you can see who can make the most frightening face.

22

Paper aeroplane

YOU WILL NEED
Sheet of paper about 20cm × 30cm
Sticky tape
Your paint box, felt pens or crayons

1

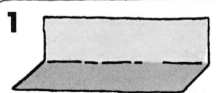

Fold the paper in half lengthwise and make a sharp crease. Unfold it again.

2

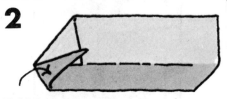

Fold the corners over at one end to meet in the middle.

3

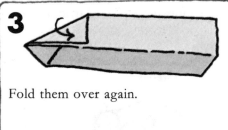

Fold them over again.

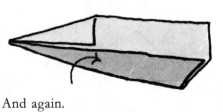

And again.

4

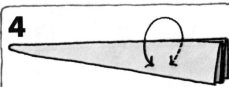

Fold the plane in half and press the creases firmly.

5

STICKY TAPE

Open out the wings and put a small piece of sticky tape across them to hold them together. With paints, felt pens or crayons decorate the plane.

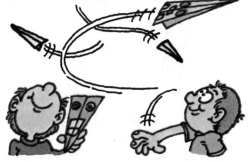

Now it is ready to fly. Get your friends to make planes too and see whose plane will fly the furthest.

23

Matchbox clock

YOU WILL NEED
Matchbox
3 paper fasteners
Thin string
Safety pin
Large button
Sheet of paper
Sticky tape
Your paint box, felt pens or crayons

1

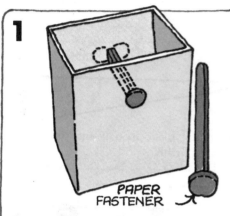

PAPER
FASTENER

You don't need the matchbox tray to make the clock, so take that out and make your clock from the matchbox cover.

Push a paper fastener through the matchbox cover near the top. Flatten the fastener on the other side.

2

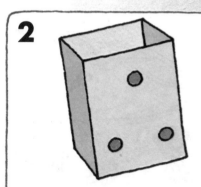

Push two more fasteners through the box – but this time near the bottom.

3

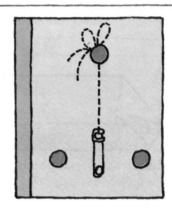

Tie a short piece of thin string to the top of a safety pin. Tie the string to the top paper fastener so that the safety pin hangs inside the box level with the two bottom fasteners.

24

4

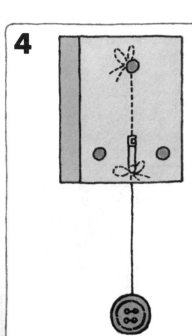

Tie another, longer, piece of string to the bottom of the pin, so that the string hangs down well below the bottom of the box. Tie a large button to the end of the string to make a pendulum.

5

TICK TOCK TICK TOCK TICK TOCK TICK TOCK TICK TOCK TICK TOCK

When you swing the pendulum your clock will tick. Tape some plain paper around the box so you can paint on a clock face.

Paper dolls

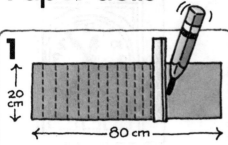

1

20 cm

← 80 cm →

Tape two or three pieces of paper together if you have not got one piece big enough.

With a ruler draw lines 5 cm apart down the paper.

2

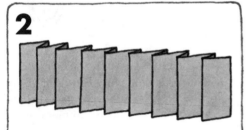

Now pleat the paper and make creases along the ruled lines.

3

Draw half a doll on the top pleat. Make sure the doll's arm goes right across the paper.

YOU WILL NEED

Sheet of plain paper about
    20 cm × 80 cm
Pencil
Ruler
Scissors
Sticky tape
Your paint box, felt pens or crayons

4

Cut out the doll cutting through all the pleats and making sure you don't cut across the end of the arm.

5

Open out the pleats and there will be several dolls holding hands. Colour in their faces and dresses.

You can make other paper people as well as dolls. You can even make a frieze of Christmas trees.

26

Cardboard jigsaw

YOU WILL NEED
Sheet of thin card
Picture cut from an old magazine or
    comic
Pencil
Scissors
Non-toxic glue
Heavy books

1

Stick the picture to the card taking care to cover the whole of the back of the picture in glue. Press it down firmly and leave to dry under a few heavy books.

2

When the glue is dry, draw a jigsaw pattern on the back of the card. Cut out the pieces.

3

See how long your friends take to put the pieces back together.

Of course you can make a jigsaw from a picture you have painted yourself. Or you can write a secret message on plain card then make the card into a jigsaw. Send the pieces of jigsaw to your friend and see if he or she can puzzle out the message.

27

Paper beak

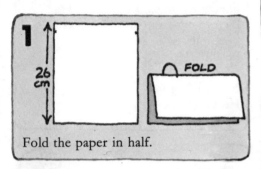

1 Fold the paper in half.

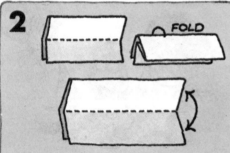

2 Fold in half again. Make a sharp crease and re-open.

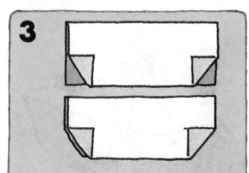

3 On one side, fold the two bottom corners up to the crease. Turn over and do the same again.

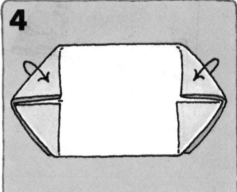

4 Now fold the thick top corners down to meet the crease.

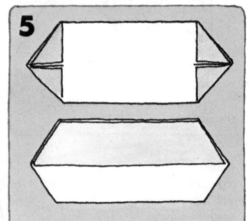

5 Fold one of the bottom flaps up to cover the top two folded corners.

28

6

Turn over and fold the other flap up.

7

SNIP SNIP

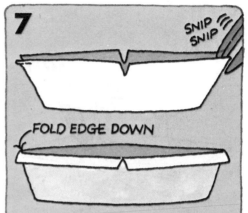

FOLD EDGE DOWN

Press all the creases firmly, then with the scissors make a tiny cut in the centre of each of the longer edges. Snip each end as well so you can fold back a little edge all round the top.

8

Push the two pointed ends together so the rim you have made becomes the edges of the mouth. Now you have a beak which will make a pecking noise when you snap it shut. Paint on eyes and decorate the beak.

Cardboard whirr

1

Draw round the top of a mug or large glass so you can cut out a circle of stiff card. Cut triangular pieces from the edge of the card.

2

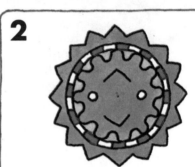

Make two small holes in the centre of the card and cut a V shaped notch above and below the holes. Decorate the card in bright colours.

Hold a loop in each hand. Twist the circle of card so that the string winds up. When you pull the string loops outwards the disc will whirr and spin.

3

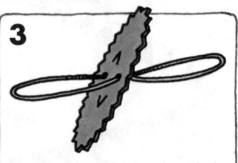

Thread a piece of string through the holes, tying the ends together, and leaving a loop of string on each side of the disc.

Newspaper tree

1

Take a double sheet of newspaper and cut it in half across the middle.

2

Tape the two halves together end to end.

3

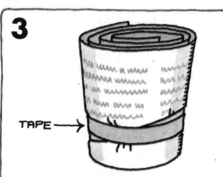

Roll the paper up into a tube. Put sticky tape around the bottom of the tube to hold it together.

4

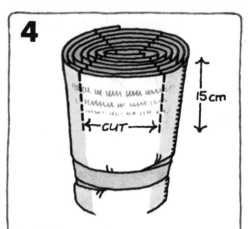

Make 4 cuts in the top of the tube. Cut about 15 cm into the paper.

5

Hold the trunk of the tree in one hand and gently pull the centre leaves upwards with the other hand.

31

Papier mâché pig

1

Prepare the papier mâché by tearing newspaper into small strips and making up the wallpaper paste in a shallow bowl according to instructions on the packet.

2

Blow up the balloon and tie the end in a knot. Carefully cover it in grease.

Soak a strip of newspaper in paste then lay it on the balloon. Add more and more strips until the balloon is covered in a layer of newspaper. (Leave the knot sticking out.) When you have completed one layer put the balloon aside until the newspaper has dried out. Add another layer and leave that to dry. You must put on six or seven layers and you must let each layer dry before adding the next.

3 FOUR DAYS LATER

When you have added enough layers, hang the balloon up by the knot in a warm place for three or four days. When you are sure the paper is really dry pop the balloon.

4

Now you have a papier mâché ball. Stick on four legs and a nose made from an egg box and glue on ears made from thin card. Now you can paint your pig.

You can carefully cut a slot in the top of the pig to make a piggy bank if you like.

Papier mâché pot

YOU WILL NEED
Old newspapers
Wallpaper paste
Grease (margarine or vegetable oil)
A plastic flower pot or yoghurt pot
Poster paints

Prepare the papier mâché by tearing newspaper into small strips and making up the wallpaper paste in a shallow bowl. Follow the instructions on the packet when you make up the paste.

2

Cover the outside of the plastic pot with grease.

3

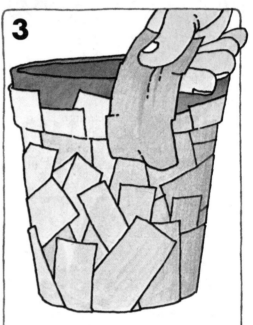

Soak a strip of newspaper in paste then lay it over the pot. Add more and more strips until the pot is covered in a layer of newspaper. When you have finished one layer you must put the pot aside until the newspaper has dried out. Then add another complete layer and let that dry. You must put on six or seven layers and you must let each layer dry before adding the next.

4

↑
LIFT

When the newspaper has really dried out, gently lift the plastic pot out and you will have a papier mâché copy. Now you can paint and decorate this paper pot with poster paints.

Papier mâché pots make nice presents, but remember you can't put anything wet inside them. Put a flower pot or yoghurt pot inside them if you want to grow plants in them.

Handkerchief parachute

YOU WILL NEED
Large handkerchief or paper napkin
Thin string
Small cork
Sheet of paper
Scissors
Sticky tape
Your paint box, felt pens or crayons
Ruler

1

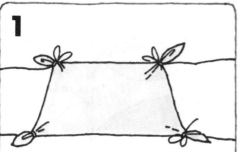

Cut four pieces of string each 30cm long. Tie one piece of string to each corner of the handkerchief.

2

Tie a piece of string tightly round the middle of the cork.

3

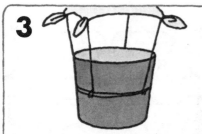

Tie the handkerchief strings to the string around the cork.

4

Draw a parachutist on the paper. Cut him out and tape him to the cork.

Drop your parachute over the banisters and watch it float down.

Jam jar snowstorm

YOU WILL NEED
Small screw top jar
Small plastic model
Glycerin (can be bought at any
    chemist)
Glitter
Non-toxic waterproof glue
Water
Teaspoon

1

LID

If the jar still has a label on it soak it off.
Make sure the inside of the lid is clean
and dry and stick a small plastic model
to it. The little figures sold as cake
decorations are ideal or use a small
plastic toy. Make sure the model will
fit inside the jar.

2

Fill the jar two-thirds full with glycerin. Top it up with water and stir in
teaspoonful of glitter.

3

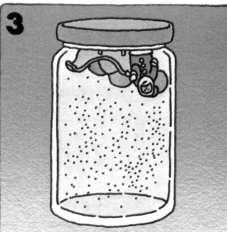

Make sure the model is stuck firmly to
the lid, then screw the lid firmly on the
jar. Turn the jar upside down and
shake well. The glittery 'snow' will fall
around the figure inside.

Handkerchief mouse

YOU WILL NEED
A large cloth handkerchief

1

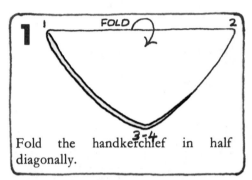

Fold the handkerchief in half diagonally.

2

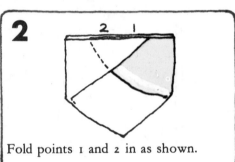

Fold points 1 and 2 in as shown.

3

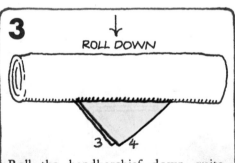

Roll the handkerchief down quite tightly, leaving points 3 and 4 as a small flap.

4

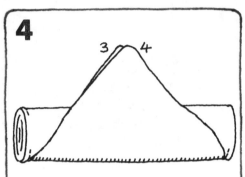

Turn the handkerchief over.

5

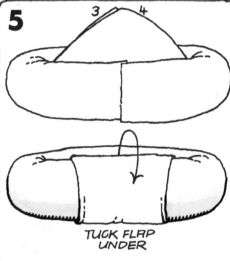

Fold the ends in and tuck the flap over and under them. Keep rolling the flap in, until you can carefully pull points 1 and 2 out.

6

Tie a knot in one end to give your mouse ears.

Sit the mouse on your hand with your fingers curled underneath the tail. Jerk the mouse up your arm with your fingers. Stop it 'escaping' with your other hand!

Puppets

You can make just one puppet for yourself and give a puppet show using the back of the settee or a chair for your puppet theatre. Or, if you have got plenty of time, you can make a whole collection of puppets and make up a puppet play. You can even make your own puppet theatre (see page 62). If your puppet talks remember to give him a funny voice!

Paper plate puppet

YOU WILL NEED
2 paper plates
Stapler or sticky tape
Scraps of wool, card etc.
Non-toxic glue
Your paint box, felt pens or crayons

1

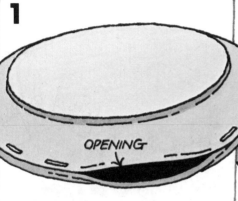

OPENING

Staple or tape the two plates together so that the bottom of both plates is on the outside. Leave a gap big enough to get your hand through.

2

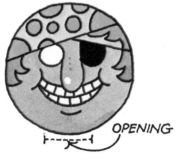

OPENING

Make sure the gap is at the bottom when you paint on a face. Remember you can stick or staple on wool and other scraps of fabric and paper to decorate the puppet.

Finger puppets

1

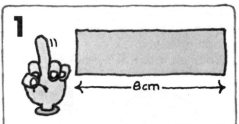

8cm

Cut a strip of paper or thin card as tall as your tallest finger and about 8cm wide.

2

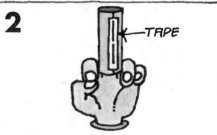

TAPE

Roll it into a tube that will fit over your finger and fasten it with tape or glue.

3

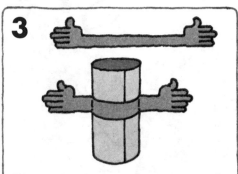

Give your puppet some arms made from a scrap of paper.

4

You can stick on pieces of paper to make a face, hair and clothes or you can draw them on.

You can make a puppet for every finger.

Or, why not make finger puppets that wriggle and walk like this! Draw an elephant without a trunk on a piece of card. Paint him and then cut him out. Cut a hole where the trunk should be and put your middle finger through the hole. When you move your arm forward across the table the elephant will move – and he can wiggle his trunk too.

Draw a body without legs on some thin card. Paint or colour the clothes and face. Cut two round holes near the bottom of the figure. Put your second and middle finger through the holes. Now your puppet can walk!

Sock or sleeve puppet

1

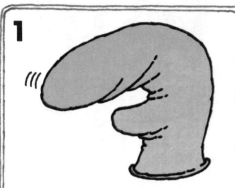

If you are using a sock, put your fingers in the toe and your thumb in the heel.

3

Now you can stick on eyes, ears and hair. Sock and sleeve puppets are good for making monsters!

2

If you are using a sleeve, tie a knot in one end. This will be the puppet's nose.

Plastic bottle puppet

YOU WILL NEED
Empty plastic bottle
Sheets of plain paper
Scraps of fabric, wool, card etc.
Scissors
Non-toxic glue
Sticky tape
Your paint box, felt pens or crayons
Pencil

1

Ask a grown up to cut off the top of the bottle.

2

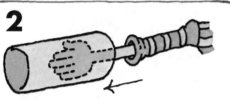

Make sure you can get your hand inside the bottle.

3

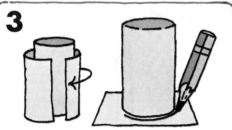

Cover the plastic bottle in paper. Remember to cover the bottom with a circle of paper as well. Draw round the bottle to get a circle the right size.

Now you can make an animal using the round end of the tube as a face or mouth. Or you can make a person using half of the tube as a face.

Paint on faces and bodies. Use scraps of wool, felt and fur for hair, manes and whiskers. Make arms from pieces of card and stick them on too.

Stick puppet

YOU WILL NEED
Strong paper bag
Stick about 40cm long
Scraps of wool, fur, felt etc.
Old newspaper
Scissors
Sticky tape
Stapler or non-toxic glue
Your paint box, felt pens or crayons
Pencil
For dress: piece of material 50cm
    square, needle and thread, ribbon

1

Draw a face on the bag. Paint or colour it.

2

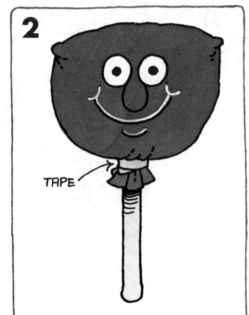

TAPE

Fill the bag with screwed up newspaper. Tape it to a stick.

3

If you have any odd scraps of wool, fur or felt you can stick or staple those on for hair, feathers etc.

4

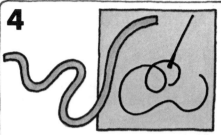

You can leave the puppet like this and just hold on to the stick and make the face move up and down. But if you have time you can make your puppet a dress. For this you need a piece of material about 50cm square, a needle and thread and a ribbon.

5

Cut one corner off the material like this. Then fold it in half and sew the straight edges together, leaving a tiny hole at the top.

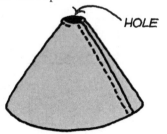

6

Push the stick with the face on it through the top of the dress. Bind sticky tape around the stick just below the neck of the dress to stop the dress slipping down. Tie a ribbon round the neck and decorate the dress if you wish.

7

Now you can move the puppet by holding the stick underneath the dress and your hand won't show.

Sock head puppet

YOU WILL NEED
An old sock
Cotton wool
Elastic band
Piece of material about 20cm × 50cm
Scraps of felt and wool
Needle and thread
Scissors
Non-toxic glue
Ruler

1

Stuff cotton wool into the toe of the sock to make a head.

2

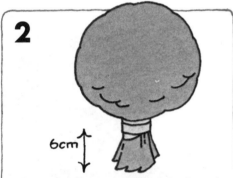

When the toe is full fasten it loosely with an elastic band. Cut off the rest of the sock so only 5 or 6cm are left hanging.

3

Now make a face on the sock by sticking on felt eyes, nose and mouth. Sew on wool for hair.

4

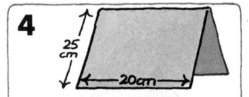

Fold the piece of material in half so that the 'right' side of the material is on the inside.

5

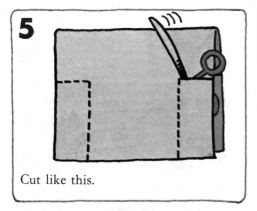

Cut like this.

6

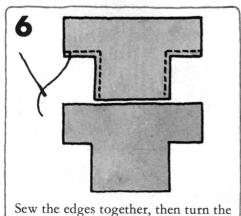

Sew the edges together, then turn the dress the right side out.

7

Make a very small hole in the top – just big enough for one finger. Push the end of the sock head through the hole.

8

Put your hand inside the dress and push your index finger up into the head of the puppet. (Loosen the elastic band if necessary). Put your thumb and little finger out through the sleeve holes. If the sleeves are too long turn them back to make cuffs.

Masks

When you wear a mask no one knows what you look like underneath so you can change yourself into a frightening monster or a beautiful princess. You can be a fierce wild animal or a little old lady. Masks are good for creating characters in plays and for playing dressing up games. You can even have a mask party.

To decorate your mask you can use coloured paper, tissue paper, crepe paper, wool, string, scraps of material, card, egg boxes, beads and anything else you can find. And you can colour your mask with paints, felt pens or crayons.

Paper bag mask

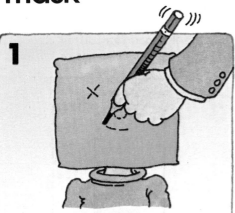

1

Put the paper bag over your head. Ask a grown up to feel where your eyes, nose and mouth are and to mark them on the outside of the bag.

2

Take the bag off and carefully cut holes where the marks come. Try the mask on again and make sure you can see and breathe properly.

YOU WILL NEED
A strong paper bag big enough to
  go over your head
Scraps of paper, cardboard, string etc.
Scissors
Stapler or sticky tape
Your paint box, felt pens or crayons

3

Now your mask is ready to decorate. You can add hair made from strips of paper and paint on eyelashes, a nose and lips. Or you can make an animal mask and stick or staple on cardboard ears and string whiskers.

Cylinder mask

1

The piece of card must be at least as wide as the distance from your shoulders to the top of your head and long enough to go round your head and overlap slightly. Have a bit extra for a hat.

YOU WILL NEED
Large piece of thin card
Scissors
Stapler or sticky tape
Scraps of paper, card, string etc.
Your paint box, felt pens or crayons

3

Now staple or stick the card into a cylinder shape.

2

Hold the card around your head and ask a grown up to mark where your eyes are. Lay the card flat and cut small holes where the marks are.

4

Paint a funny face with 'false eyes' in a different place from your own eyes so the mask gives you a much bigger head than usual!

5

And you can give your mask a hat. Cut a circle of card slightly larger than the top of your cylinder. Stick it on to the top of the mask, as the base of the hat.

6

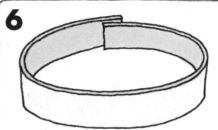

Cut a long strip of card – long enough to go round your head. Make it into a ring and tape it to the base of the hat. You can make different faces and different hats to suit them. Have a look at the section on hats starting on page 111 for some more ideas.

Domino

A domino is a small mask that just covers the top of your face. People used to wear them to parties called masquerades. Bandits sometimes wear them too!

YOU WILL NEED
Piece of thin card about
    20cm × 10cm
Elastic
Scissors
Your paint box, felt pens or crayons

1

Hold the card over your eyes and ask a grown up to mark where your eyes and nose are with a pencil.

3

Round off the ends of the mask and make a small hole in each side. Thread elastic through to hold the mask on. Now you can paint and decorate the mask.

2

Lay the card down and cut out holes for the eyes and nose.

Tie-on mask

YOU WILL NEED
Piece of card as large as your face
Elastic
Scissors
Stapler or sticky tape
Scraps of paper, card, string etc.
Your paint box, felt pens or crayons

1

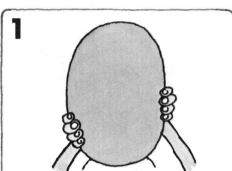

Cut out an oval of card large enough to cover your face.

2

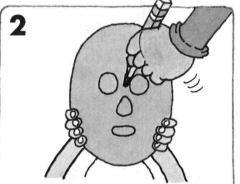

Hold the oval up to your face and ask a grown up to mark where your eyes, nose and mouth are.

3

Lay the mask down and cut holes where the marks come. Make two small holes on the edge of the mask just above the eye holes and thread elastic through.

Now you can decorate your mask. Don't forget you can tape or staple on hair, ears etc.

Cardboard box creations

It's amazing how many toys and games you can make from a few strong cardboard boxes.

There are only two problems about working with strong cardboard boxes. The first is that they are difficult to cut. You really need a sharp knife to cut them so ask a grown up for help.

The second problem is painting them. It takes a lot of paint to cover a big cardboard box and the paints and brushes in your paint box probably aren't suitable. Of course you don't have to paint your cardboard box toys, but if you want to, ask if you can buy a tin of emulsion paint and borrow a large brush. Be very careful when you are using the emulsion paint. Paint the boxes out of doors or put lots and lots of newspapers on the floor.

Dolls' house

YOU WILL NEED
3 or more cardboard boxes of about
   the same size
Large piece of cardboard
Scissors
Non-toxic glue
White emulsion paint and large
   brush
Your paint box, felt pens or crayons

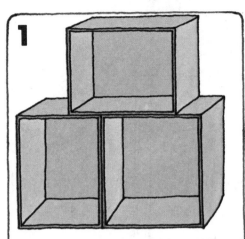

1

Stick the boxes together so the open sides all face the same way.

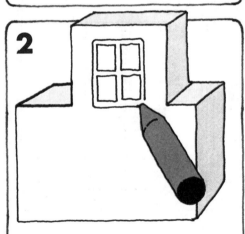

2

Paint the outside of the boxes with white emulsion paint. When this is dry draw windows and other details on the closed ends using your own paints, felt pens or crayons.

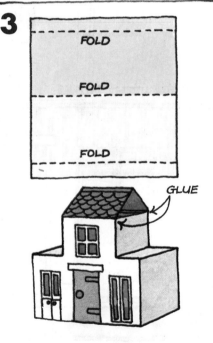

3

FOLD

FOLD

FOLD

GLUE

To make the roof you need a piece of cardboard just over twice the size of the top of your dolls' house. Fold the card down the centre to make a sloping roof. Paint on tiles and stick the roof to the boxes.

Now you can decorate the inside of the dolls' house. Paint the walls of the rooms with the white emulsion paint or 'wallpaper' them with pretty coloured paper. Remember to paint windows on the inside too. Paint a picture of a garden behind French windows in one room.

Dolls' house furniture

Furnishing your dolls' house is great fun. You can make furniture out of almost anything. Here are some ideas but I expect you can think of lots more.

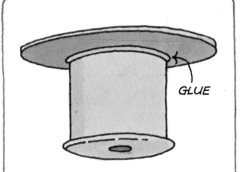

GLUE

Make a table from a square or circle of card stuck on to a cotton reel or cork.

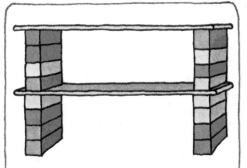

Make shelves from strips of cardboard and toy bricks (or make 'bricks' from Plasticine). Put tiny toys on the shelves as ornaments.

GLUE ON BACK

Make chairs or stools from cotton reels or corks covered in scraps of material. Or cut a cardboard tube into rings and cover them. You can add backs to any of these chairs by glueing on pieces of cardboard.

59

Make easy chairs and a settee by sticking together matchboxes. Then paint them or cover them with scraps of material.

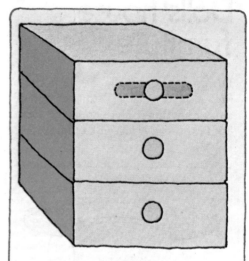

Make a chest of drawers from matchboxes glued together. Make handles by pushing paper fasteners through the front of each drawer.

Make beds from small boxes turned upside down with scraps of material for sheets and blankets.

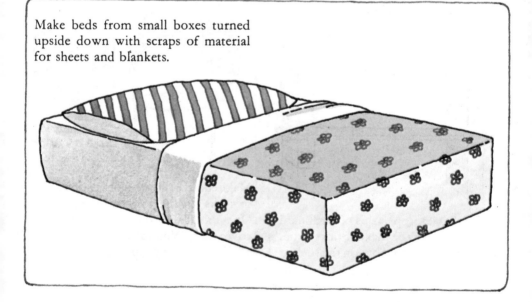

Small boxes covered in paper and painted make excellent cookers, fridges, televisions, wardrobes etc.

Don't forget to add the finishing touches with carpets, made from pieces of material, pictures cut from old magazines, mirrors made from silver foil stuck on tiny pieces of cardboard and lampshades made from coloured paper. Hang the lampshades from the ceilings by threading cotton through the top of the shade and taping the cotton to the ceiling. Make a lamp by putting a paper shade over a cotton reel or cork.

Puppet theatre

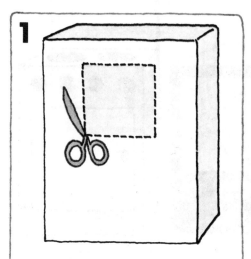

1

Ask a grown up to cut a square hole in the box, as shown.

YOU WILL NEED
A large cardboard box
Emulsion paint and large brush
Scissors

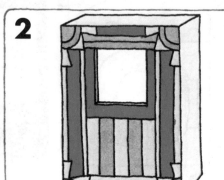

2

Paint the outside of your theatre, get inside with your puppets, and you are ready to give a puppet show.

3

If you like you can make your box into a television instead and make up your own programmes.

Animal costume

1

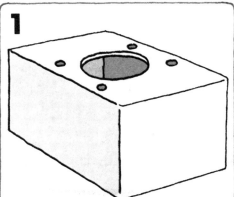

Ask a grown up to cut a hole in the middle of the bottom of the box, big enough to fit around your waist. Ask them to make four tiny holes around the centre hole as well.

YOU WILL NEED
One large box
Some thick cord or string
Scraps of thin card, string etc.
Scissors
Emulsion paint and large brush
Your paint box, felt pens or crayons

2

Thread cord through the small holes so you have two straps. Try the box on, putting the cord over your shoulders. Make sure the straps are the right length for the box to hang at your waist.

3

Now you can decide what animal you want to be. When you have decided, paint the box all over in an appropriate colour emulsion paint. Then you can stick on cardboard ears, a string tail etc. and draw on a face using your own paints, felt pens or crayons.

63

Robot costume

1

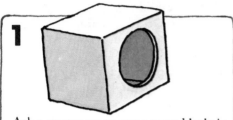

Ask a grown up to cut a round hole in the front of the 'head' box.

YOU WILL NEED
One cardboard box big enough to go over your head
One cardboard box big enough to go over your body
Tin foil or non-toxic silver paint
Cotton reels, bottle tops, corks etc.
Scraps of thin card
Scissors
Non-toxic glue
Felt pens or crayons

2

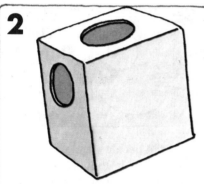

And ask them to cut arm holes and a neck hole big enough to put your head through in the 'body' box.

Remember to walk like a robot – with stiff arms and legs – and make robot noises!

3

Now you can paint the boxes with silver paint or cover them in tin foil. Stick on bottle tops and cotton reels and corks covered in tin foil for the knobs. Make cardboard dials and stick them on too.

Aeroplane

YOU WILL NEED
6 large cardboard boxes
Large piece of thin card
Scissors
Non-toxic glue or sticky tape
Emulsion paint and large brush
Your paint box, felt pens or crayons

1

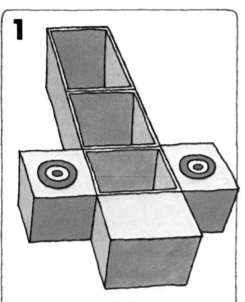

Glue or tape the boxes together like this. You don't have to paint your aeroplane all over but if you do it's best to use emulsion paint. You can use your own paints or crayons to paint on your own airline insignia.

2

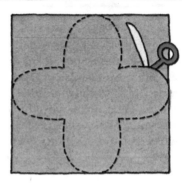

Cut out a propeller from a piece of cardboard and stick it on the front. Paint controls inside the box where you sit.

Train

1

YOU WILL NEED
At least four large cardboard boxes
String
Small pieces of thin card
Non-toxic glue or sticky tape
Green emulsion paint and large
  brush
Your paint box, felt pens or crayons
Scissors

Glue or tape two boxes together like this to make the engine. Paint them all over with green emulsion paint. Make wheels and a window from scraps of thin card, paint them in bright colours using your own paints, felt pens or crayons and stick them to the engine.

2

Now the other boxes can be carriages – one for each of your friends. And everyone can decorate his or her own carriage. Make a small hole in the ends of each carriage. Thread string through a hole in two boxes and tie knots on the insides. Join all your carriages together like this.

Castle

YOU WILL NEED
Large cardboard box
3 or 4 smaller boxes
3 or 4 cardboard tubes or plastic
  bottles
Scraps of coloured paper
Pins
Sticky tape
Non-toxic glue
Grey emulsion paint and a large brush
Your paint box, felt pens or crayons
Cup or glass
Scissors
Pencil

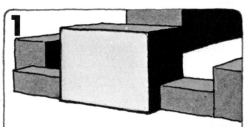

1 Take the large box, turn it upside down and paint it grey all over. Stick the other boxes around it and paint them with grey emulsion paint as well.

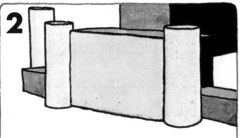

2 Add towers made from plastic bottles or cardboard tubes. Paint them too.

3 Now you can decorate the castle. Use your own paints or crayons to add battlements, windows and doors.

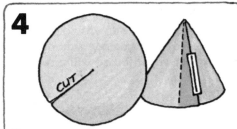

4 Put paper cones on top of the towers. Make them by drawing round a cup or glass. Cut out the circle and make one cut into the centre. Slip one side of the cut paper under the other and fasten with sticky tape.

Make little paper flags and tape them to pins. Stick the pins in the top of the towers.

If you've got some toy soldiers line them up outside the castle.

Garage

YOU WILL NEED
Small flat cardboard box
Piece of thick cardboard bigger than
   the base of the box
Smaller piece of thick card
4 or 5 matchboxes
Plain paper
String
Scissors
Sticky tape
Non-toxic glue
White emulsion paint and large
   brush
Your paint box, felt pens or crayons

1

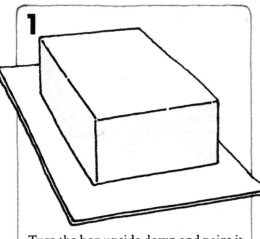

Turn the box upside down and paint it white all over. Paint one side of the large sheet of cardboard white too.

2

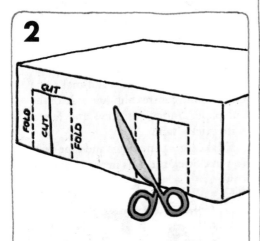

Ask a grown up to make cuts like this in one side of the box. Fold the flaps back carefully to make doors.

3

Make a ramp to lead to the garage roof from the cardboard, and tape it to the box. Stick the garage on to the large piece of cardboard which will be the forecourt.

68

4

Now you can add the finishing touches. Make petrol pumps from matchboxes covered in paper and painted. Tape string to one side of the matchboxes to look like a petrol hose.

Use your own paint box, felt pens or crayons to put windows and signs on the garage and paint lines on the forecourt.

Now you can put your toy cars into the garage.

Film set

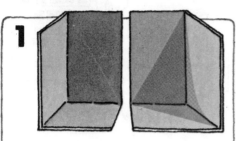

1

Ask a grown up to cut two of the sides off each box.

YOU WILL NEED
2 large cardboard boxes about the
    same size
Sticky tape
Your paint box, felt pens or crayons
Scraps of paper, card, small boxes,
    egg boxes, plastic bottles etc.
Scissors

2

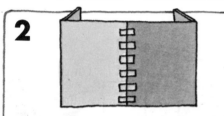

Tape the cut boxes together at the back.

3

Now you can paint the scenery. You could paint a country scene and put your toy farm animals on the set. Make a farmhouse from a small box.

4

Or make a zoo. Draw some animals on the sides of the box and use model animals as well. Make cages by drawing bars on small boxes.

5

You can make a space scene if you like. Paint a picture of how you imagine the surface of Mars, around the inside of the boxes. Make a space ship from a plastic bottle and 'space scenery' from egg boxes.

If you need models for your film sets – the next section has lots of ideas for making people, animals and monsters!

You can even use the papier mâché dough (see page 75) to make 'hills and valleys' on the floor of the film sets.

Village

You can make a whole village from different sized cardboard boxes. Get all your friends to help – perhaps they can each make a house or shop. Just paint and colour the up-turned boxes to make the buildings and add roofs made of thin card. If the boxes are difficult to paint, cover them in paper first.

Models and modelling

If you want models for your film sets (page 70), dolls for your dolls' house (page 57), soldiers for your castle (page 67) or if you just want to make some little animals or people and you haven't any Plasticine or clay, here are some ideas.

Salt dough models

This is good for making small items such as dolls' house dinners, tiny figures and little ornaments.

YOU WILL NEED
Plain white flour
Salt
Cooking oil
Water
Mixing bowl
Poster paints
Varnish and brush

1

Mix equal amounts of salt and flour in a bowl. Add a little cooking oil and enough water to make a dough. Knead until the dough is soft and stretchy. Now you can make whatever you like.

2

If you can't use the oven, make a dough using less salt – three parts of flour to one part salt. Add paint or food colouring to the salt and flour before you add the water because you will not be able to paint these models.

Salt dough keeps for a long time in an airtight plastic bag or tin.

When you have made your models, leave them to dry for a day or two, then ask a grown up if you may put them on the bottom rack in the oven at a low heat. Leave them in the oven for several hours until they are very hard. Make sure they don't burn.

Now you can paint and varnish the models.

Papier mâché models

To model with papier mâché you need to make a softer mixture than for covering moulds and it takes longer to prepare.

WALLPAPER PASTE

1

Tear about 40 sheets of newspaper into very small pieces and put all the pieces in a bucket. Cover the paper with water and let it stand for 24 hours. Then pour off and squeeze out the surplus water. Add a cupful of wallpaper paste made up according to the instruction on the packet.

2

Knead the mixture until it feels like soft clay.

Now you can make all kinds of models. Leave them to dry in a warm place and after a few days you can paint them. If you want to make a large model, use a box as a base. You can varnish the models too if you like.

Cotton reel animals

This is a nice, quick way to make animals for a toy farm or zoo.

1 Draw animal fronts and backs like these on thin card. Make sure the front and back are about the same size. Colour them in and cut them out.

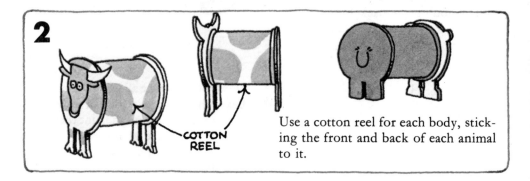

2 COTTON REEL

Use a cotton reel for each body, sticking the front and back of each animal to it.

Egg box animals

Pieces of egg box can be used to make animals, insects and monsters! Stick on pieces of card for feet, wings etc. Paint the animals and use pipe-cleaners for antennae and legs.

77

Yoghurt pot people

YOU WILL NEED
Yoghurt pots
Sheets of plain paper
Scraps of card and wool
Sticky tape
Non-toxic glue
Your paint box, felt pens or crayons
Scissors

1

Turn the clean yoghurt pots upside down and cover them with paper. Fasten the paper around them with sticky tape.

2

Paint on faces, add wool for hair and cut out thin card shapes for arms, shoes and hats.

Making music

Lots of things can be made into musical instruments with very little effort. Collect together some friends and you can make a band – but you had better ask permission first, because your band will probably be very noisy!

Kitchen music makers

Saucepan lids make good cymbals.

A saucepan and wooden spoons make a drum.

Make a water xylophone from jam jars or glasses. Fill the jars with different amounts of water. Remember the more water in the glass the lower the note it will produce when you hit it with a spoon.

Two wooden spoons banged together become rhythm sticks.

Comb buzzer

YOU WILL NEED
Comb
Tissue paper

Wrap a comb in a piece of tissue paper.
Put it to your lips and blow gently.

Rattle

YOU WILL NEED
Tin or yoghurt pot with a reusable
  lid
Rice or dried peas

Just fill the tin or pot half full with rice
or dried peas and fix the lid on tightly.
Now you have a rattle.

Guitar

YOU WILL NEED
Shallow tin
Elastic bands

Stretch the elastic bands over the tin
and pluck or strum them.

Tooter

Whistle

YOU WILL NEED
Long cardboard tube
Tissue paper
Elastic band

YOU WILL NEED
Sheet of paper
Scissors

1

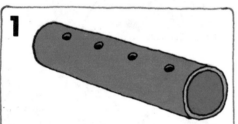

Ask a grown up to punch some holes in the tube.

1

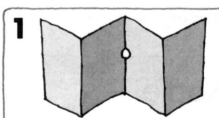

Cut a long strip of paper. Fold it in four and open it out again. Tear a small hole in the centre fold.

2

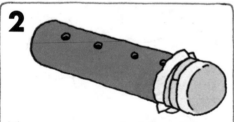

Then cover one end of the tube with tissue paper held in place with an elastic band.

2

3

Blow into the open end.

Hold the whistle to your mouth like this and blow.

Foil top tambourine and shaker

To make a tambourine, thread the bottle tops or circles of foil in groups of three or four and attach them loosely to the edge of the paper plate.

YOU WILL NEED
Paper plate
Stick
Milk bottle tops or small circles of tin foil
Needle and cotton
Sticky tape

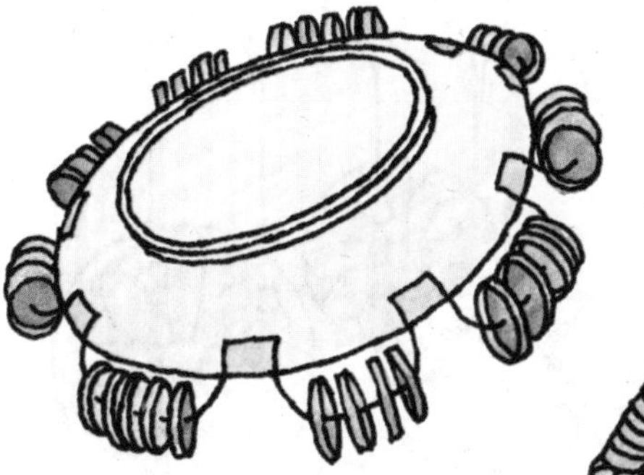

To make the shaker thread the foil tops on to lengths of cotton – about 20 tops on each strand. Tie the cotton to the stick. Shake the stick to make a noise.

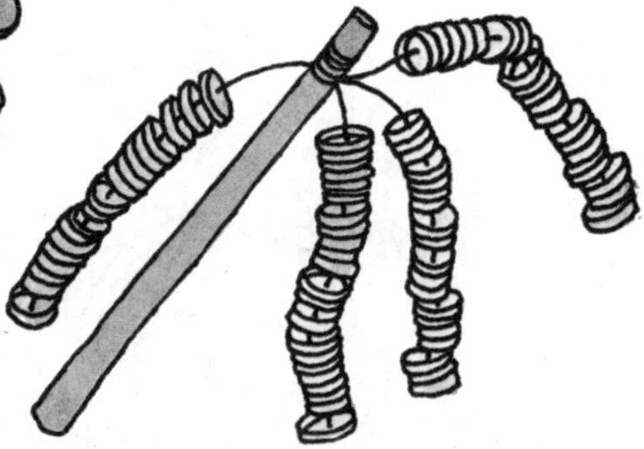

Funny flowers

A vase of paper flowers will brighten up any room, and here's how to make some flowers.

Tin foil rose

1

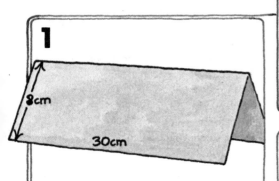

Fold a strip of foil in half lengthwise.

2

Roll the foil up loosely. Then pinch one end together.

3

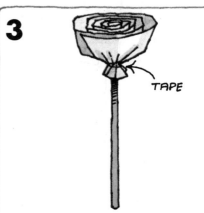

TAPE

Tape the end of the rose securely — taping on a thin stick at the same time. You can then bend the head of the rose forward.

Paper plate flower

YOU WILL NEED
Small paper plates (or plate-sized circles of cardboard)
Thin sticks
Different coloured sheets of crepe paper or tissue paper
Scissors
Sticky tape
Non-toxic glue
Your paint box, felt pens or crayons
Thin card
Pencil

1

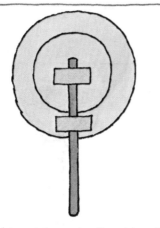

Tape a thin stick to the flat side of a paper plate.

3

If you want to make a more detailed flower, cut out lots of different coloured petal shapes from tissue or crepe paper.

2

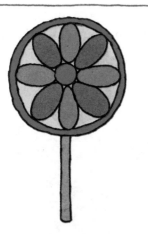

You can make a very simple flower by just painting a flower on to the plate.

4

Tape or glue these petals to the paper plate. Stick them round the rim first and then work inwards.

5

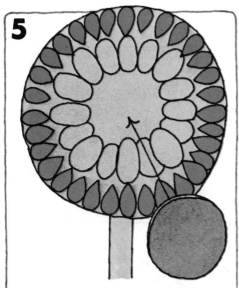

Cut out a small circle of card and cover it with coloured paper and stick it in the centre of the flower.

6

You can make magic flowers with petals of all different colours or you can make flowers that look like the flowers in your garden.

7

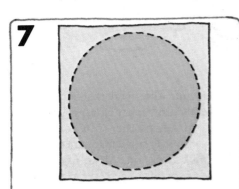

Cut out a square of tissue or crepe paper a little bigger than your paper plate.

8

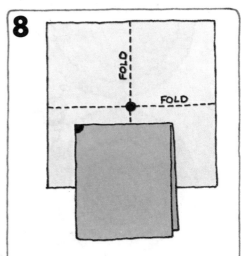

Fold the square into four, marking the centre.

9

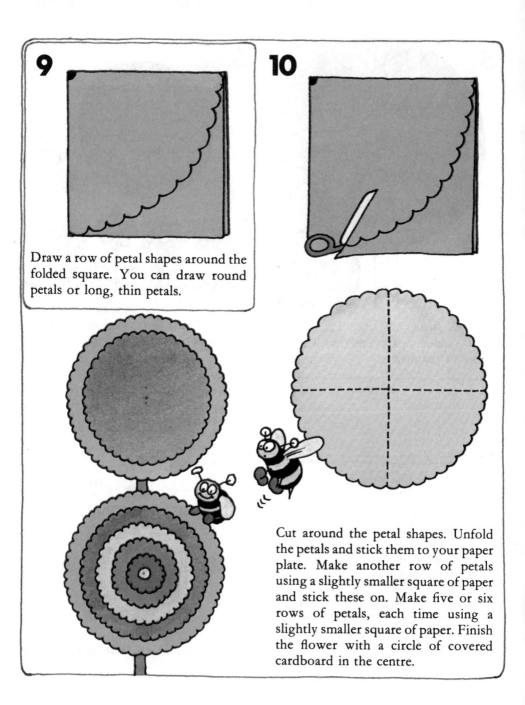

Draw a row of petal shapes around the folded square. You can draw round petals or long, thin petals.

10

Cut around the petal shapes. Unfold the petals and stick them to your paper plate. Make another row of petals using a slightly smaller square of paper and stick these on. Make five or six rows of petals, each time using a slightly smaller square of paper. Finish the flower with a circle of covered cardboard in the centre.

Lollipop tree

1

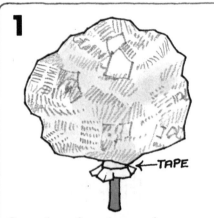

←—TAPE

Crumple a few sheets of newspaper into a ball. Push a thin stick into the ball of newspaper and hold it in place with sticky tape.

YOU WILL NEED
Tin foil
Old newspaper
Yoghurt pot
Earth or sand
Thin stick
Scraps of plain and coloured paper
Scissors
Sticky tape
Non-toxic glue
Your paint box, felt pens or crayons

3

Cover the yoghurt pot with foil and fill it with earth or sand. Push the stick into the sand.

2

Cover the newspaper ball in tin foil.

Now you can decorate the tree. You could make it into a fruit tree – sticking on apples or oranges you have cut out and painted – or you could have a flowery tree. Cut out and colour paper flowers then stick them to the tree.

Tissue carnation

YOU WILL NEED
Different coloured paper
  handkerchiefs
Thin sticks
Stapler
Scissors
Sticky tape
Ruler

1

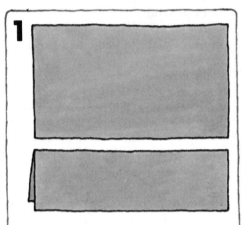

Open out one tissue then fold it in half lengthwise.

2

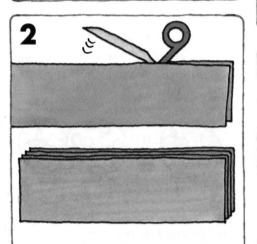

Cut along the fold. Because each handkerchief has two layers of paper you should now have four layers of tissue.

3

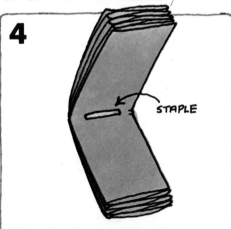

Pleat the layers of tissue together making each pleat about 1.5 cm wide.

4

STAPLE

When the tissue is pleated, fold it in half. Staple along the fold.

5

Holding the stapled end, very gently separate the layers of tissue. They will fluff out to form a carnation.

6

If you want to put the carnations in a vase, tape them to thin sticks.

These flowers make a very pretty decoration when you are wrapping up a special present. Or you can wear them in your hair!

Badges, beads and other bits

All these items are fun to wear and easy to make.

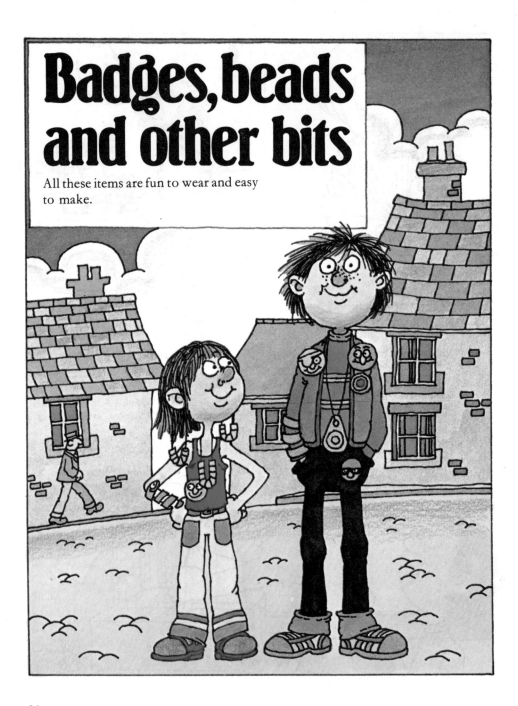

Badges and brooches

YOU WILL NEED
Thin card
Safety pins
Eggcup
Scissors
Sticky tape
Scraps of felt, odd beads, sequins,
    shells etc
Non-toxic glue
Your paint box, felt pens or crayons
Pencil

1

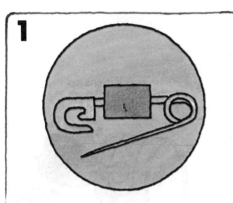

Put an eggcup on a piece of thin card and draw round it. Cut out the circle of card and tape a safety pin to the back of it.

2

Now you can paint or decorate your badge however you like – perhaps with your name or just with a funny face or a pattern.

3

If you have some small pieces of felt you can cover the cardboard base in felt and make felt faces.

4

If you want to make a brooch, you can stick beads, sequins or even small shells to the cardboard base.

Beads

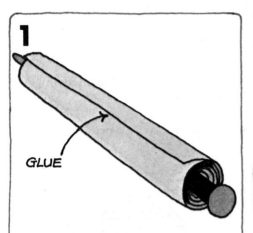

1

GLUE

Roll a piece of paper round a knitting needle and stick the end down along its complete length.

YOU WILL NEED
Sheets of plain paper about
    20cm × 30cm
Knitting needle
Thin string or wool
Ruler
Scissors or knife
Non-toxic glue
Your paint box, felt pens or crayons

3

Now you can paint the beads or draw patterns on them with felt pens or crayons.

2

When the glue is dry, slide the knitting needle out and cut the rolled up paper tube into lots of 'beads'.

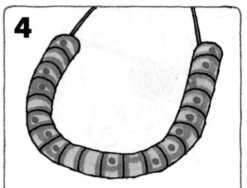

4

When you have made enough beads, thread them on to a piece of thin string or wool and tie it round your neck like a necklace.

5

You can make some earrings to match the necklace. Tie a loop of wool or thin string big enough to go over your ear.

6

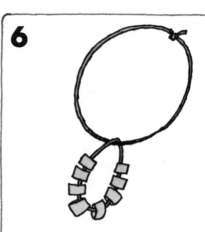

Thread a few paper beads together and tie them into a ring. Fasten the ring of beads to the loop of wool and slip the loop over your ear. Make another earring exactly the same so you have a pair.

Pendant

YOU WILL NEED
Thin card
Ribbon or thin cord
Scissors
Sticky tape
Non-toxic glue
Beads, sequins, small shells, scraps of felt etc.
Your paint box, felt pens or crayons
Pencil

1

Cut out a cardboard shape like this. Draw round it and cut out another shape exactly the same.

2

Stick a small loop of ribbon or cord to one of the pieces of card with sticky tape.

3

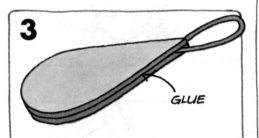

GLUE

Now stick the two pieces of card together so the loop is on the inside.

4

Decorate the pendant by sticking things on to the card or by painting it. Thread a ribbon or cord through the loop and tie the ends. Slip the pendant over your head.

Bangle

YOU WILL NEED
Thin card about 4cm × 22cm
Tin foil
Scissors
Sticky tape
Non-toxic glue
Your paint box, felt pens or crayons

1

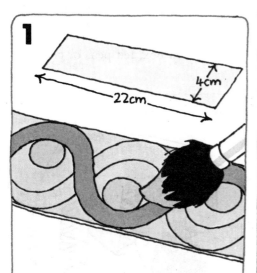

To make a very simple bangle, paint a pattern on the card.

2

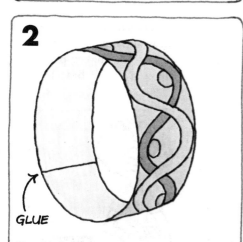

GLUE

Bend it into a circle and tape or glue the ends together.

3

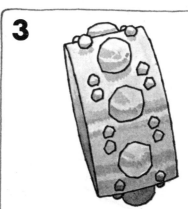

You can make a 'silver' bracelet by covering the card in tin foil. Crush some scraps of foil into little balls and stick them to the outside of the bracelet for 'jewels'.

Snake bracelets

YOU WILL NEED
Long cardboard tube from the inside
 of a roll of kitchen paper
Scissors
Your paint box, felt pens or crayons

1

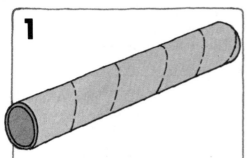

If you look at the tube carefully you
will see that it has a spiral seam line
running around it.

2

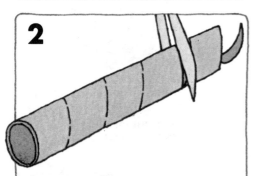

Cut along this line so you are left with a
curly strip of card.

3

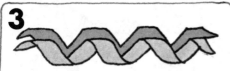

Cut this strip in half all along its length
so you have two 'snakes'.

ROUND OFF

Round off the ends of both bracelets so
you have a head and tail. Paint on some
snake eyes and some snakey patterns.
Now you have a snake bracelet for
each arm!

Salt dough jewellery

If you make the dough described on page 74, you can use it to make beads and pendants.

YOU WILL NEED
Plain white flour
Salt
Cooking oil
Water
Mixing bowl
Large needle
String or ribbon
Poster paints
Varnish and brush
Pencil or coin

1

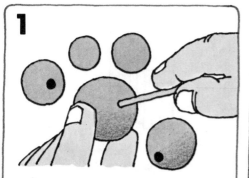

Roll the dough into small balls to make beads and use a large needle to make a hole through the centre of each one before it dries.

2

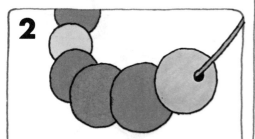

When the beads have been baked dry you can paint them – and varnish them if you wish – before threading them on to a string to make necklaces, bracelets or earrings.

3

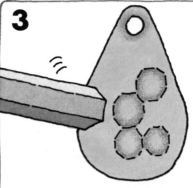

You can make a pendant out of sour dough and print a pattern on it. Make a pendant shape and then use the end of a pencil or a coin or whatever you like, to make an impression in the dough. Remember to make a hole in the top before the dough is baked dry so you can thread it on a string or ribbon.

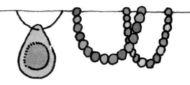

Fan

You can make a fan to match the rest of your jewellery.

YOU WILL NEED
Piece of plain paper about
   60cm × 20cm
Sticky tape
Ruler
Your paint box, felt pens or crayons

1

If you can't find a piece of paper big enough, stick several pieces together with sticky tape.

3

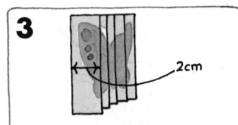

2cm

Now pleat the paper. Make each pleat about 2cm wide. Draw lines to pleat along if you find it easier.

2

Decorate the paper. Flowers, birds and butterflies are pretty on fans, or you can colour the fan in stripes about 2cm across. Paint both sides of the fan.

4

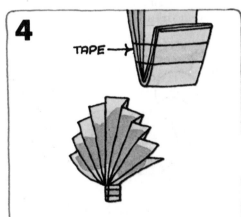

TAPE →

Push the pleats together at one end. Bend the end up and put sticky tape around it to make a handle. Spread out the fan.

Shell and stone presents

It's fun to collect shells and pebbles when you go to the seaside and it's easy to turn them into pretty shell and stone ornaments.

Shell animals

YOU WILL NEED
An assortment of shells
Strong non-toxic glue
Varnish and brush
Tiny beads for eyes, string for tails
 pipe-cleaners for antennae etc.

Which animals you make depends on the shells you have, but here are some ideas to get you started. Try and think of some more animals to make yourself.

When the glue is dry, varnish the shells carefully. This will keep their colours nice and bright.

Shell box

YOU WILL NEED
Small box or tin with a removeable
   lid
Strong non-toxic glue or putty
Varnish and brush
Lots of small shells

Make sure the lid of the box or tin is
clean and dry. Lay the shells on the lid
and try out different patterns. When
you have found a pattern you like,
stick the shells on to the lid. Or if you
have some putty you can cover the top
of the box with it and stick the shells
into that. When the glue or putty is
dry, varnish the shells.

A shell box makes a nice present. You
can put something inside to make it an
extra-special gift.

Pebble paperweights

At the seaside and beside some rivers you can find beautiful smooth pebbles. If you paint pictures on these stones they make very pretty ornaments or paperweights.

Always wash the pebbles first and let them dry. If you want, you can draw your design on in pencil first and then paint over it. You can make patterns or pictures. When the paint is dry, cover the stone in a thin layer of varnish.

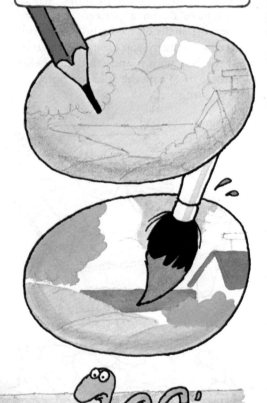

You might find some stones which already look like funny creatures. With some stones, see if you can make a monster!

Mobiles

A mobile is a decoration that moves as the air moves. You don't need to hang a mobile in a draught though. All rooms are full of air currents that will move your mobile gently round and round. Here are some ideas for simple mobiles that are very easy to make.

Remember that babies like mobiles. You can hang a mobile above the baby's cot and he or she will be able to watch the figures spinning round.

One string mobile

YOU WILL NEED
Thin card
Thin string
Saucer
Scissors
Your paint box, felt pens or crayons

1

Draw round a saucer on the card.

2

Cut out the circle and draw a happy face on one side of it.

3

Draw a sad face on the other side.

4

Make a small hole in the top of the circle. Thread some string through and hang your mobile up. The face will change from happy to sad as the mobile turns.

Of course you don't have to make faces. You can make a single string mobile of a flower, fish or bird.

Heads, bodies and legs

YOU WILL NEED
Thin card – 40cm × 10cm
Thin string
Pencil
Ruler
Scissors
Your paint box, felt pens or crayons

1

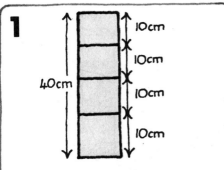

Mark off four 10cm squares down the card with a pencil.

2

Now draw a person on the card. You must draw the head on the top square, the arms and body down to the waist on the second square, the rest of the body and legs down to the knees on the third square and the rest of the legs and the feet on the bottom square. Turn the card over and draw another figure in the same way. Make the two figures as different as possible.

3

Now cut the card into four squares and make a small hole in the top and bottom of each piece. Join the squares to each other with separate pieces of thin string. Hang the mobile up and as it turns you will see some funny mixed-up people!

Hanging in a line

You can hang any pieces of card, one beneath the other, and they will turn slowly as long as the pieces of card are joined in the middle. Paint the pieces of card and then join them with thin string.

YOU WILL NEED
Thin card
Thin string
Scissors
Your paint box, felt pens or crayons

Shiny mobile

1

Using an eggcup to draw round, cut out twelve small circles of thin card and twenty-four circles of tin foil. Stick a foil circle on both sides of each piece of card.

YOU WILL NEED
Thin card
Tin foil
Plastic drinking straw
Thin string
Needle and thread
Scissors
Eggcup
Non-toxic glue
Pencil

2

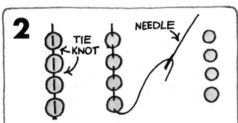

TIE KNOT

NEEDLE

Thread the circles together in fours using a needle.

3

Thread a length of thin string through a plastic drinking straw and tie the ends of the string together.

4

Tie the rows of foil covered circles to the straw. Hang up your mobile and watch the foil circles catch the light as they move.

Round mobile

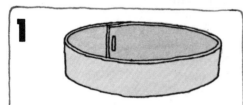

1

Staple or tape the ends of the card together to make a circle.

2

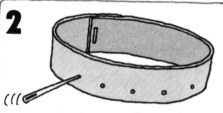

With a needle, make a small hole every 6cm around the edge of the circle.

3

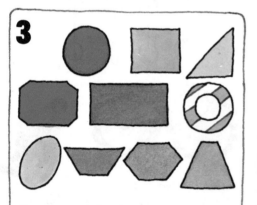

Cut out 10 different cardboard shapes. Colour and decorate them.

YOU WILL NEED
Thin card about 6cm × 60cm
Thin card for shapes
Needle and thread
Thin string
Sticky tape or stapler
Your paint box, felt pens or crayons
Scissors
Ruler

4

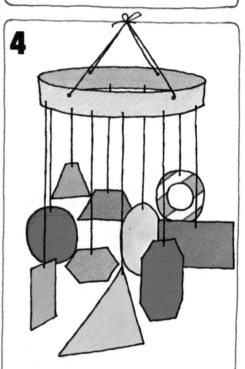

Using a needle and thread hang the shapes from the holes in the circle of card. Use a different length of thread for each shape. Make four small holes in the top of the circle and attach thin string to hang the mobile up.

Hats

Here are some ideas for basic hat shapes. But what really makes a hat special is the way you decorate it; you can paint it, stick on tassles, flowers or pom-poms or just make it out of pretty coloured paper.

A competition for the funniest, biggest or best decorated hat is a good party game and a hat can add the finishing touch to a fancy dress costume.

Some of these hats need rather large squares of stiff paper to make them. If you do not have any sheets of paper large enough, stick smaller pieces together with sticky tape – or try using sheets of brown wrapping paper.

Pointed hat

A tall pointed hat can be made into a witch's hat, a clown's hat or a princess's hat.

1

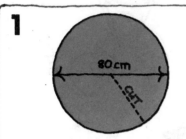

Cut once into the centre of the circle of card.

2

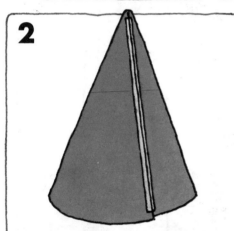

Fold inwards and overlap the edges of the paper until you have made a cone. When you have checked that the cone will fit on your head, tape the edges together. Now you can paint and decorate the hat.

YOU WILL NEED
A circle of card or stiff paper about
    80cm in diameter
Sticky tape
Non-toxic glue
Ruler
Your paint box, felt pens or crayons
Scissors

To make a witch's hat paint the cone black and stick on foil covered stars. (See page 128 for how to make stars.)

To make a clown's hat paint the cone in a bright colour and stick on tissue paper balls for pom-poms – or make the tissue paper flowers described on page 90 and use those for pom-poms.

To make a princess's hat you need a thin head scarf. Paint the cone in a pretty colour and then stick the scarf by one corner to the top of it.

Crown

1

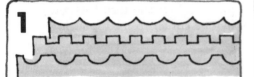

Cut a pattern along the top of the card.

Paint the crown and decorate it with
'jewels' made from tin foil, scraps of
coloured paper etc.

2   TAPE

Tape the ends of the card together.
Your crown is now ready to wear.

114

Red Indian headdress

If you can find enough real feathers you can use those to make the headdress. If not make some feathers out of thin card. Cut out feather shapes and fringe the sides to make them look 'feathery'.

YOU WILL NEED
Thin card about 10cm wide and long
   enough to go round your head
Scissors
Sticky tape
Feathers
Your paint box, felt pens or crayons

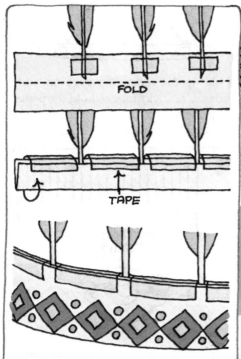

FOLD

TAPE

Tape the feathers to the top half of the card. Fold the bottom half of the band up to cover the ends of the feathers and fix with sticky tape. Decorate the band. Tape the band into a circle.

If you want to make a squaw's headdress you can make a headband in exactly the same way but use only one feather.

Newspaper hat

This is a very easy hat to make. If you make it and like it perhaps you could find a piece of plain paper big enough to make it from as you can't paint or colour newspaper very easily.

YOU WILL NEED
Sheet of newspaper
Sticky tape
Strip of tissue paper
Scissors

1

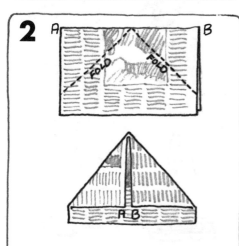

Take a large sheet of newspaper or a double sheet from a small newspaper. Fold it in half.

2

Fold the two top corners so that they meet in the middle.

3

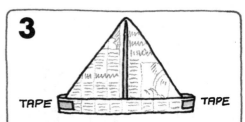

Fold up the remaining edge on both sides. Use sticky tape to hold the paper in position.

4

You can decorate this hat by making a tissue paper tassle. Cut a strip of tissue paper in a fringe all along one edge. Roll up the strip and screw the uncut edge together tightly. Let the cut ends hang free. Stick this tassle into the top of the hat.

Party hat

YOU WILL NEED
Stiff paper 65–70cm square
Sticky tape

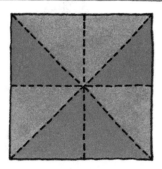

1

The exact size of the square of paper depends on the size of your head. The best thing to do is to experiment by making the hat with a sheet of news-paper first.

Fold the paper in half crossways and then diagonally and then unfold it again so that you leave creases like this.

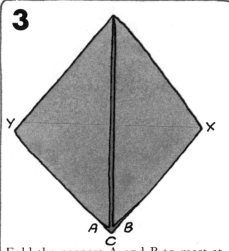

3

Fold the corners A and B to meet at point C.

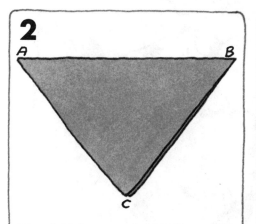

2

Now fold the paper in half diagonally.

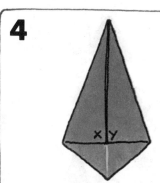

4

Then turn the paper over and fold the corners X and Y into the centre.

5

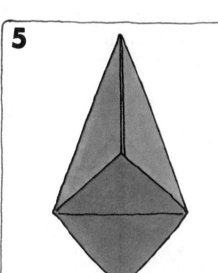

Turn the paper over again and fold up the bottom flaps of paper leaving one piece hanging.

6

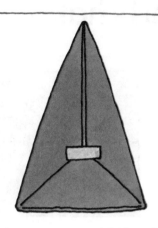

Turn the paper over and fold up the last flap. Fasten the upturned flaps with sticky tape to hold the hat firmly together. Decorate the hat.

Pirate's hat

YOU WILL NEED
50–60cm square of stiff paper
Your paint box, felt pens or crayons
Scissors

1

The exact size of the square of paper depends on the size of your head. The best thing to do is to experiment by making the hat with a sheet of newspaper first.

Make diagonal folds across the square to leave creases like this.

3

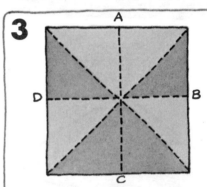

Now your paper will have these creases.

2

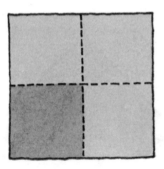

Turn the paper over and make crossways folds to leave creases like this.

4

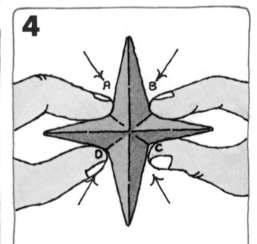

Push the creases of the squares towards each other like this.

5

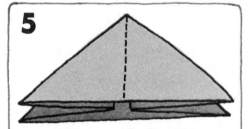

Flatten the paper to this shape.

6

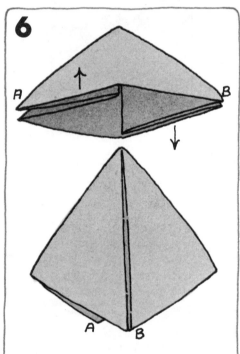

With your right hand hold the bottom three thicknesses together on the right-hand side. With your left hand hold the top three thicknesses together on the left-hand side. Twist so the front centre fold ends up on the left-hand side.

7

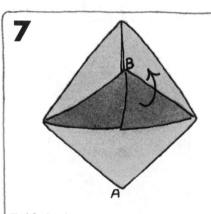

Fold the loose corners plus one layer from beneath to the top of the hat.

8

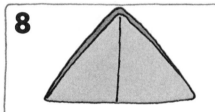

Turn the hat over and do the same on the other side.

9

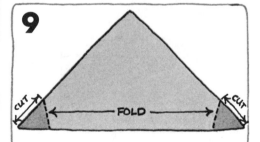

Make a small cut then press up the corners. Decorate with a skull and crossbones.

Hair

You can make 'hair' to wear under your hats by taping strands of wool or strips of crepe paper to the hat itself or to a band of card.

You can make very striking hair from strips of tin foil. Cut thin strips about 40cm long then run the blunt edge of the scissors down the strip. It will curl up into a lovely ringlet. Attach these to a band for 'space-age' hair!

If you have got a lot of spare wool you can make two plaits. These will look good attached to the squaw's head-dress (see page 115).

1

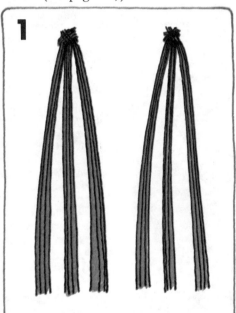

Cut the wool into 30cm lengths. Divide it into six equal amounts. Take three of the six lengths and tie them together at the top.

2

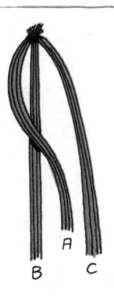

Plait the wool by bringing the left-hand side strand of wool over the centre strand. This means the centre strand becomes the new left-hand strand.

3

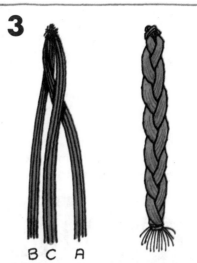

Now take the right-hand side strand over the centre strand – now the centre strand becomes the new right-hand strand. Repeat this until you reach the bottom. Tie the ends tightly and repeat the whole process to make the second plait.

4

Fix the plaits to a headband with a piece of wool threaded through the top.

Decorations

You needn't wait until Christmas time to make decorations. It's fun to decorate the house for a birthday party, or if there is a carnival, fair or fete in your town you can make some decorations to brighten up the floats or stalls.

Spinning spiral

YOU WILL NEED
Sheet of coloured paper or foil
A dinner plate
Pencil
Scissors
Needle and cotton

1

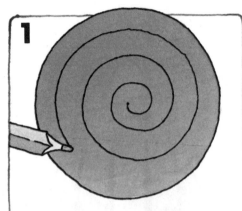

Put the plate on the coloured paper or foil and draw round it. Cut out the circle of paper and carefully draw a spiral on it beginning at the centre.

3

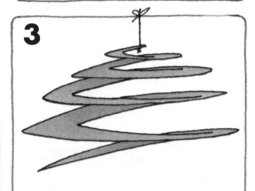

You can make a spinning spiral out of plain paper and colour it in if you like.

2

Cut along the line you have drawn. Sew a piece of cotton through the centre of the spiral to hang it up by.

125

Paper lantern

YOU WILL NEED
Piece of coloured paper about
   35cm × 20cm
Scissors
Sticky tape
Ruler

1

Cut a thin strip from one end of the oblong of paper. Put the strip carefully aside to use later.

2

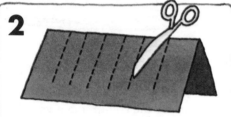

Fold the oblong in half lengthwise. With the scissors, make a row of cuts through the folded side of the paper. Make sure the cuts stop at least 2cm from the edge of the paper.

3

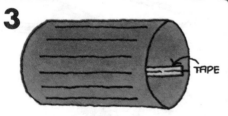

Open out the paper and bend it into a circle, taping the edges together.

4

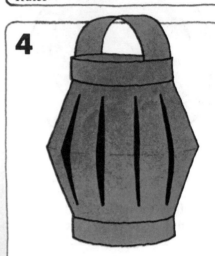

Make a handle from the strip of paper you cut off earlier. Hold it in place with sticky tape.

Paper chain

1

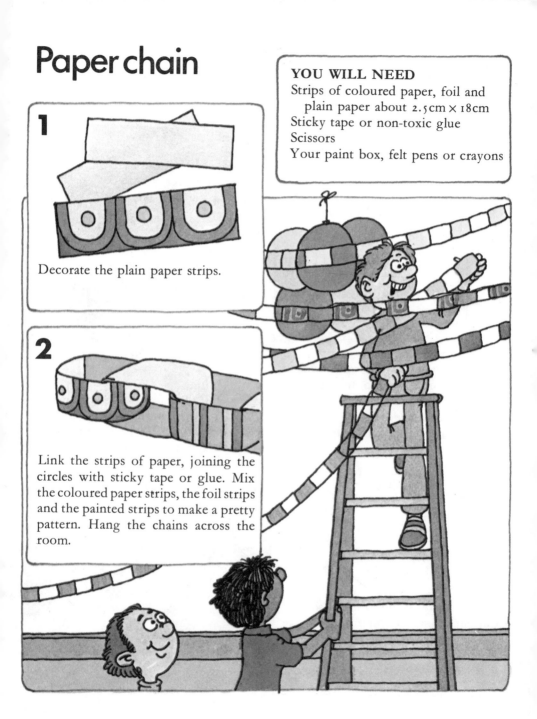

Decorate the plain paper strips.

2

Link the strips of paper, joining the circles with sticky tape or glue. Mix the coloured paper strips, the foil strips and the painted strips to make a pretty pattern. Hang the chains across the room.

127

Stars

Stars are a pretty decoration at any time of the year. Ask permission first and perhaps you will be allowed to stick a pattern of stars on your bedroom ceiling.

YOU WILL NEED
Thin card
Plain paper, tin foil or coloured
    paper
Pencil
Ruler
Needle and cotton
Plate or saucer
Your paint box, felt pens or crayons
Scissors

1

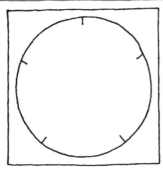

Draw a circle on the card using a saucer or small plate to draw round. Cut out the circle. Make five marks round the outside of the circle at roughly the same distance apart.

3

Decorate the stars using paints or pens, or cover them in silver or gold paper. If you want to hang the stars up, push a needle and cotton through one point and hang the star up by the thread.

2

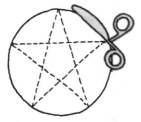

Join the marks using a ruler as shown. Cut out the star. If you want to make lots of stars use this first one as a pattern for the rest by drawing round it.

Snowflakes

1

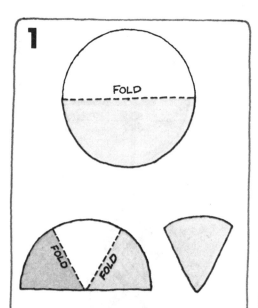

Lay a saucer or small plate on the paper and draw round it. Cut out the circle of paper. Fold it in half and then into thirds.

2

Cut the pointed top off the cone shape and cut different shaped notches in the sides and bottom of the cone. Open out the paper and you have your snowflake.

YOU WILL NEED
Sheet of plain paper
Scissors
Pencil
Saucer or plate

3

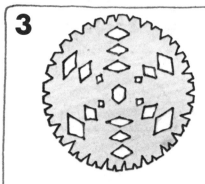

Snowflakes can be stuck on to windows for a Christmas decoration or use them as doilies on plates to make your party table look pretty.

Paper bell

YOU WILL NEED
Sheet of coloured paper
Scissors
Pencil
Saucer or plate
Ribbon

1

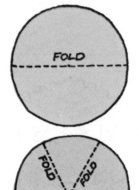

FOLD

FOLD FOLD

Put a saucer or small plate on the paper and draw round it. Cut out the circle of paper. Fold it in half and then into thirds.

2

Make cuts from side to side of the cone as shown. The closer the cuts are to each other the better.

3

Open the paper out very carefully and stretch the rings gently downwards. Hang the bell up using a piece of ribbon threaded through the top.

Icicles

1

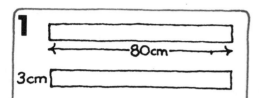

Cut strips of foil or coloured paper about 3cm wide and 80cm or more long.

2

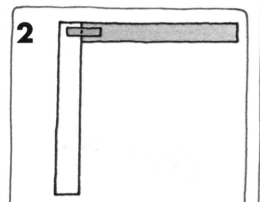

Lay two strips on a flat surface and tape the end of one strip to the end of the other so the strips are lying at right angles.

3

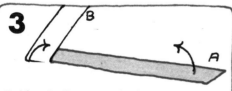

Fold strip B over strip A.
Then fold A over B.

4

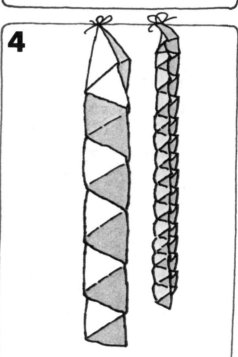

Continue folding the strips over each other until all the paper is folded. Fasten the ends together with sticky tape. Using a needle, thread cotton through the top to hang up your icicle. You can hang these decorations in the window, from the ceiling or from your Christmas tree.

Snowman

YOU WILL NEED
Small cardboard tube
Cotton wool (the sort that comes in
 a sheet)
Ribbon
Thin card
Non-toxic glue
Your paint box, felt pens or crayons
Pencil
Scissors

1

Cover all but the top 2cm of the tube in cotton wool, sticking it down with glue.

2

Make a hat from a circle of thin card. To do this draw round the end of the tube and then draw a second, slightly larger, circle around that one.

3

CUT OUT

Cut out the large circle and then cut the small circle out of the middle so you are left with a ring. Paint the ring black and slip it over the top of the tube so it rests on the cotton wool. Paint the top of the tube and the small circle black too. Stick the circle to the top of the tube.

4

Tie a ribbon round the snowman's neck to make a scarf. Cut out, paint and stick on cardboard eyes, nose, mouth and buttons.

If you are having a Christmas (or winter) party you can use the snowmen as table decorations. Stand one by each plate with a name tag to show whose place it is.

JOHN

SARAH

Christmas tree

YOU WILL NEED
A large circle of thin cardboard
Scraps of coloured paper
Wrapped sweets
Sticky tape
Non-toxic glue
Your paint box, felt pens or crayons
Scissors

1

Make one cut into the centre of the circle of cardboard and then make a cone. Tape the edges together, then paint the cone green all over.

2

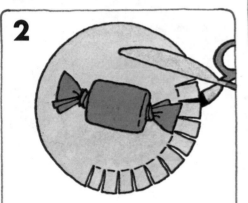

Cut out small circles of coloured paper and make little cuts around the edges of each circle to make a fringe. Stick small wrapped sweets in the centre of each circle of paper. Then stick the circles to the tree.

This is a nice decoration to put in the middle of your Christmas dinner table. Or you can hide little presents underneath it.

Father Christmas

YOU WILL NEED
A circle of thin cardboard
Cotton wool
Sticky tape
Non-toxic glue
Your paint box, felt pens or crayons
Scissors

1

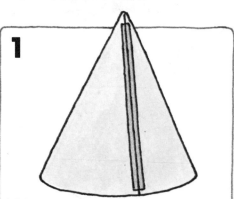

Make one cut into the centre of the circle of cardboard and form a cone. Tape the edges together to hold the card in place.

2

Draw on a face and paint the rest of the cone red.

3

Stick on cotton wool for hair and whiskers.

135

Painting, printing and pictures

Before you begin any painting or printing projects always have plenty of newspaper to cover the table – and the floor if you are doing something very messy. And wear old clothes or a painting smock: a big, old shirt worn back to front makes a good smock.

I expect you have lots of ideas about the kind of pictures you want to paint, but here are a few of the more unusual pictures you can create.

Easy pictures

YOU WILL NEED
Sheets of plain paper
Your paint box, felt pens, crayons or
  wax crayon
Coins

One of the easiest pictures of all to make is a scribble picture. With a crayon scribble all over a sheet of paper. Fill in the scribble in different colours and you will have a very unusual pattern.

Another sort of easy picture to make is a 'draw-round' picture. See if you can create a whole picture just by drawing round a few coins. Have a competition to see who can think of the most unusual things to create using the coins.

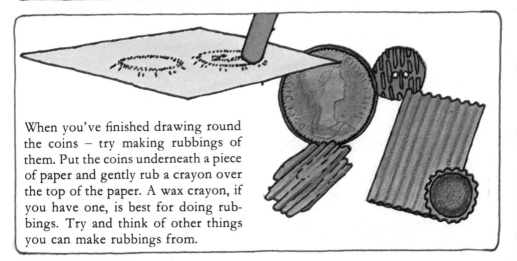

When you've finished drawing round the coins – try making rubbings of them. Put the coins underneath a piece of paper and gently rub a crayon over the top of the paper. A wax crayon, if you have one, is best for doing rubbings. Try and think of other things you can make rubbings from.

Messy pictures

It is fun to make a mess sometimes – just make sure you clear up afterwards! The best thing about messy pictures is that no one can ever be sure how they are going to turn out.

YOU WILL NEED
.Sheets of plain paper
Drinking straw
Thin card
Flour
Water
Your paint box
Old comb or fork
Mixing bowl
Scissors
Spoon

Put a lot of runny paint on a piece of paper. Blow at it through a straw so the paint moves about. That way you can make an interesting 'blow painting'.

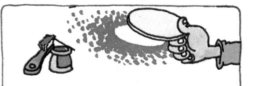

Make a spatter painting by this method: hold a brush full of drippy paint over a sheet of paper. Tap the brush hard and watch the paint spatter! If you like you can cut out some card shapes, place them on top of your paper, spatter the paint over them and then pick the shapes up to leave a pattern.

To make a fold painting, make a crease down the middle of a piece of paper by folding it in half. Put large, wet splodges of paint on one side of the paper. Fold the paper in half and press the two sides together firmly. Open the paper and see what kind of pattern you've made.

If you want to make a paste picture you have to make a flour and water paste first. Just slowly add water to a small amount of flour in a bowl, stirring all the time until you have a thick paste. Colour the paste with paint then spread the mixture all over a thick piece of paper. Now make patterns in the paste – with your fingers, with an old comb, with a fork – or with anything else you can think of. You could use an old glass or even your whole hand.

Giant pictures

Don't always paint a small oblong picture – make a huge one! If you can't find big sheets of paper tape small ones together. Giant pictures are extra fun because you can work on them with your friends.

YOU WILL NEED
Sheets of plain paper
Sticky tape
Your paint box, felt pens or crayons
Drawing pins

A frieze is a long decorative painting or sculpture which runs along a wall. You can easily make a frieze by taping four or five pieces of paper together in a line. Then all you have to do is decide on a subject for your frieze – you could make a seaside frieze, an underwater frieze, a space monster frieze – whatever you like. Paint on a background across all the paper then everyone can paint in the details they choose.

If you can find 26 pieces of paper you can make an alphabet frieze – this is a nice present for a younger brother or sister.

A mural is a painting as big as a wall! It's not easy to find that much paper but ask around for old pieces of wallpaper or sheets of thick wrapping paper. It's best to make a mural in the summer when you can work outside. Ask if you may tack the paper to a wooden fence with drawing pins – then you can paint on a really large scale.

One of the things you could put on your mural is a life-size self-portrait. Get a friend to draw round you then you can colour yourself in!

Printing

You can print with almost anything – the end of a cotton reel, vegetables, leaves, kitchen implements – even your hands and feet. Printing is just a method of putting paint or ink on one surface and pressing that surface on to paper. Printing is useful because it means you can make the same shape over and over again which is useful for making patterns and borders.

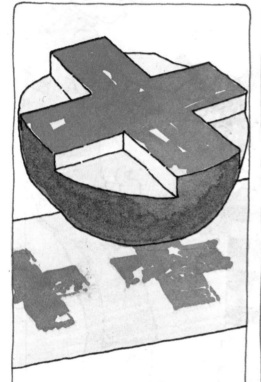

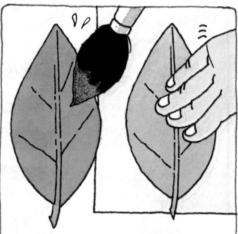

YOU WILL NEED
2 or 3 potatoes
Potato peeler
Collection of different shaped leaves
Sheets of plain and tissue paper
Non-toxic paints

A potato is good to print with because you can cut a raised pattern in the potato. Cut the potato in half. Then dig out a simple design on the flat ends, brush on paint and then press the potato on to your paper. A potato print on tissue paper in thick paint makes unusual wrapping paper.

To make a leaf print, collect as many different leaves as you can. Take each leaf in turn and paint all over one side of it. Don't use too much paint. Press the painted side of the leaf down on to your paper.

Don't forget to try experimenting with other ways of printing.

Mosaic

On the card lightly sketch in with a pencil an outline for your picture. Instead of colouring the picture in – cut out small squares of coloured paper from old magazines and stick them on until the picture is filled in.

YOU WILL NEED
Piece of thick paper or card
Old magazines
Scissors
Non-toxic glue
Pencil

Collages

A collage is a picture made from odds and ends stuck on to a base. Collages are great fun to make because you can use such a variety of items for each picture.

Pasta collage

YOU WILL NEED
Strong piece of card for base
Different shapes of pasta
Pencil
Non-toxic glue

Sketch an outline of your picture or pattern on the card and then fill in the picture by sticking on pasta shapes.

Magazine collage

YOU WILL NEED
Strong piece of card
Old magazines
Non-toxic glue

Cut pictures from old magazines and stick them on to your piece of card to make a pattern. It could be a collage of faces, or of food, or of cars – whatever you like.

Use your imagination and make a junk collage. Try and think of all the things you could stick to your card to create a collage – scraps of material and wool, bits of egg box, old Christmas and birthday cards, feathers, leaves, nuts and bolts, string etc.

Time to tidy up!

Do you keep getting into trouble because your room is a mess? It isn't much fun tidying up but if you make some of these things you might find tidying up a bit easier! They make good presents for untidy friends too!

Toy box

All you need to do is paint the box all over – inside and outside if you have enough paint – and then decide how you want to decorate it.

You can stick on cardboard ears and make your box into an animal. You can tape on crepe paper to make feathers or a mane. Or you can stick on pictures cut from an old magazine or old birthday or Christmas cards.

YOU WILL NEED
Strong cardboard box
Emulsion paint and large brush
Thin card, crepe paper, pictures etc.
Scissors
Sticky tape
Non-toxic glue
Your paint box, felt pens or crayons

Make enough boxes to keep all your toys in, and don't forget to make a box to keep all those useful bits and pieces you need to make the things in this book. There is a list of odds and ends that it is useful to collect, at the beginning of the book.

Desk tidy

YOU WILL NEED
2 long cardboard tubes
2 plastic bottles
20cm square of strong cardboard
2 sheets of pretty wrapping paper
Scissors
Sticky tape
Non-toxic glue

1

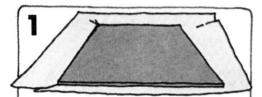

Cover the square of cardboard with wrapping paper.

2

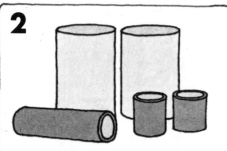

Ask a grown up to cut the top off the two washing-up liquid bottles. And ask them to cut one of the cardboard tubes in half.

3

Cover the bottles and tubes in the wrapping paper, fastening it around them with sticky tape.

4

Stick the bottles and tubes to the covered card. Now you have a desk tidy where you can put pencils, pens, paint brushes, scissors, pins, paper clips etc.

Walltidy

1

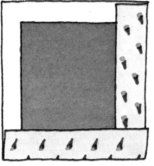

Cover one side of the piece of cardboard with wrapping paper.

2

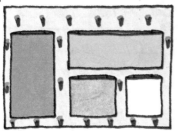

Cut the flaps from the envelopes and stick the envelopes to the board.

YOU WILL NEED

Large piece of strong cardboard about 60cm × 40cm – one side of a cardboard box is ideal
4 or 5 different sized envelopes
Sheet of pretty wrapping paper
Thin string
Sticky tape
Non-toxic glue

3

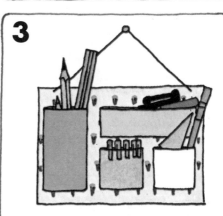

Make two small holes in the top edge of the board and thread a piece of string through. Now you can hang up your wall tidy. Use it above a desk to hold pens, pencils, paper clips etc. or use it in the bedroom to hold combs, hair slides etc.

Clothes peg clip

YOU WILL NEED
A clothes peg
Thin card
Scissors
Non-toxic glue
Your paint box, felt pens or crayons

1

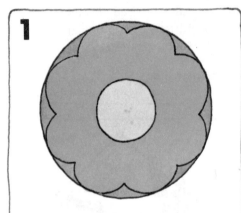

Cut out a flower shape in thin card. Make sure it is bigger than the clothes peg.

2

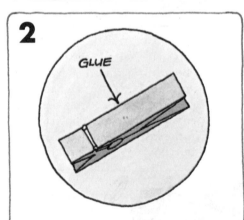

Paint or colour in the flower. Stick the clothes peg to the back of it.

3

Now you have a giant paper clip you can use to hold papers together.

Book ends

If your books are lying around with torn covers and dog-eared pages why not make a pair of book ends so you can stand the books up on a shelf.

YOU WILL NEED
2 tins with reusable lids
Enough sand or earth to fill them
Plain paper
Sticky tape
Scissors
Your paint box, felt pens or crayons

1

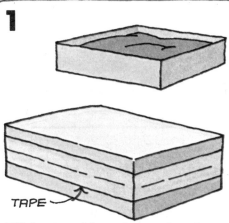

TAPE

Fill the tins with sand or earth and put the lids back on very tightly. To make sure the lids stay on, put sticky tape around and over them.

3

Draw and colour in patterns on the paper. If you are using rectangular tins you can decorate the paper to make them look like books.

2

Now wrap a piece of paper around each tin. Cut it to fit, but leave a small overlap so you can tape the paper around the tins after you have decorated it.

4

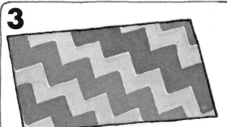

Fasten the paper round the tins with sticky tape and your book ends are ready to use.

Book jacket

1

Lay the book you want to cover open
on the paper. Cut V-shaped pieces
from the paper so that the points of the
Vs fall at the corners of the spine. Push
the remaining two strips of paper
down the back of the spine.

FOLD

2

Fold the paper into the book at the top and bottom at both ends of the book.

3

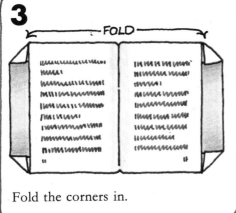

Fold the corners in.

4

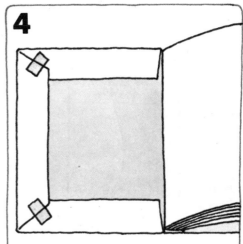

Fold the paper in at the sides and fix the corners of the cover down with sticky tape.

Now you can design your own book jacket. Don't forget to put the title on!

Book marks

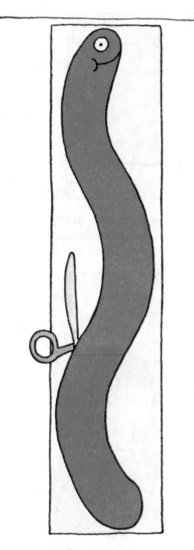

Draw a worm on thin card. Colour it in then cut it out. Now you've got a book worm book mark.

YOU WILL NEED
Thin card
Envelope
Scissors
Your paint box, felt pens or crayons
Pencil

An even easier way to make a book mark is to cut off the corner of an envelope. Colour it in a bright colour. Slip this bookmark over the corner of the page you want to mark.

THEY GAVE US SHAKESPEARE

Frontispiece.
Dedicatory inscription on St. Mary Aldermanbury memorial, London.

THEY GAVE US SHAKESPEARE

John Heminge & Henry Condell

by

Charles Connell

Shakespeare, at length thy pious fellows give
The world thy works.

Leonard Digges

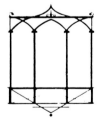

ORIEL PRESS
STOCKSFIELD
BOSTON   HENLEY   LONDON

First published in 1982
by Oriel Press (Routledge & Kegan Paul)
Branch End, Stocksfield,
Northumberland, NE43 7NA

Set in Times Roman
Printed and bound in Great Britain
by Knight & Forster, Leeds

ISBN 0 85362 193 4

To
Frederick Cleary,
whose idea it was,
who provided the title, and
who helped considerably with
the research.

Acknowledgements

The author and publisher gratefully acknowledge the assistance of all who have helped in the preparation of this book. Our special thanks are due to The Guildhall Library of the City of London, The Shakespeare Birthplace Trust at Stratford-upon-Avon, the Governors of Dulwich College and the President and the Archivist of Westminster College, Fulton, Missouri.

Photographic Credits

Plates II, III, V, VI, VII
    The Guildhall Library

Plates IV, X, XI
    The Shakespeare Birthplace Trust

Plates IX, XII
    Dulwich College Art Gallery

Plates XIV, XV
    Westminster College, Fulton, Missouri

Contents

x

Illustrations

xi

THEY GAVE US SHAKESPEARE, HEMINGE & CONDELL

I

.....All the world's a stage
And all the men and women merely players.

Shakespeare

ONE OF THE MANY London churches destroyed
by the Great Fire of 1666 and rebuilt under the
direction of Sir Christopher Wren was that of St.
Mary-the-Virgin, Aldermanbury. Dating back to the twelfth
century and possibly earlier, the original church had a cloister
running round the churchyard, and it is generally believed
that the lower part of the steeple survived the Fire and was
incorporated into Wren's new creation.

The Wren church, finished in 1677, is interesting for
various reasons, but especially in view of what happened to it
after its destruction in the London *blitz* during the Second
World War. In memory of Sir Winston Churchill, the ruins
were collected together and transported to Fulton, Missouri.
There they were reassembled to serve as a chapel at
Westminster College.

The first church to be built on the site, however, has an even
more fascinating history, for it is closely linked with two men
whose rich contribution to our literary heritage has never
been equalled. Very little is known about them; few people,
indeed, have heard of them, Yet without their devotion,

assiduity and indefatigable efforts, the world would have been poorer by what is generally referred to as the Shakespeare canon. At a time when actors were still widely considered to be little better than strolling vagabonds and dramatic works hardly regarded as serious literature, this astonishing pair thought fit to collect together and publish in one volume the plays of their fellow actor, William Shakespeare. About Shakespeare, we are informed by many of his commentators, few real facts emerge, but this lack of information has not deterred hundreds of biographers, critics and scholars from producing a mass of books about him. Even less is known about the two men who preserved Shakespeare for posterity and references to them are discouragingly rare. It is, however, the author's firm contention that they should be known, valued and remembered, not only because they are connected with the Shakespeare story, but because without them that story could never have been properly told.

As for their own place in the Shakespearian legend, it will be found that alongside the hard core of truth there exists a fair measure of guesswork and speculation. The reader, therefore, must be patient and be prepared to accept without quibbling a certain amount of evidence that perhaps would not stand up in a court of law. What must be borne in mind throughout our investigations is the established fact that our two 'witnesses' were contemporaries of Shakespeare, co-actors with Shakespeare and, most important of all, friends and intimates of Shakespeare.

Even at the outset of our study, we are confronted with a disturbing uncertainty. Their names, as spelled in 1896 by a fervid admirer, Charles Clement Walker, are John Heminge and Henry Condell. But once we start digging into the records, we find such variations as Hemings, Heminges, Hemmings, Hemminge and Heming, while alternatives to Condell are Condall, Cundell, Cundall and Condye.

Biographical dictionaries fail to give the birth dates of either, although *The Dictionary of National Biography* suggests that John Heminge was born round about the year 1556. They died within three years of each other — Condell in 1627 and Heminge in 1630. Exactly when they became involved with the theatre is not known, but records show that they were both listed in the King's Company, previously called the Lord Chamberlain's Company, in 1597 or 1598.[1] Before that, however, Heminge had already begun his theatrical career with Queen Elizabeth's Company, transferring in 1593 to Lord Strange's Men and possibly becoming associated with the Chamberlain's Company on its reorganisation in 1594.

As for his 'fellow', Henry Condell, if, as is generally supposed, as 'Harry' he played Ferrex in *Envy* and a Lord in *Lechery* in the cast of *Seven Deadly Sins,* he must have been a member of Lord Strange's Company in or about 1590. It has been suggested that he was Heminge's apprentice before 1589 and that he played female parts in Shakespeare's early plays, but there is nothing to support such conjectures.

Both men must have had a genuine love of the theatre and acting. They also came from the same neighbourhood, Aldermanbury, and worshipped in the same parish, that of St. Mary-the-Virgin, where they eventually became church-wardens. They are buried there, as are their wives, and it is there that they have received fitting recognition for their labours on behalf of their comrade and fellow Thespian, William Shakespeare. The church, as we know, is now in America, but the site was acquired by the City Corporation in 1966 and converted into a quiet garden.

The Chairman of the Metropolitan Public Gardens Association, Mr. F. E. Cleary, was asked if he could do something to improve the garden at St. Mary Aldermanbury and it was while he was inspecting the site that he came across a statue of William Shakespeare that had been set there to

3

commemorate John Heminge and Henry Condell and their efforts to bring about the publication of Shakespeare's plays. The thought that he was standing on the very spot where Heminge and Condell used to meet their old friend Shakespeare, prompted Mr. Cleary to look into the history of the dramatist's fellow actors. The more he discovered about the two men and the monumental task they undertook, the more he realised that they had received little credit for their remarkable achievement. He was particularly surprised to find that they hardly figured in the 1964 Shakespeare quatercentenary celebrations. The present volume, triggered off by Mr. Cleary's infectious enthusiasm, is an attempt to set the record right and to give the playwright's two most devoted friends a place in the Shakespeare story to which they are truly entitled.

Purchased as an open space by the City Corporation on April 16th, 1970, the garden of St. Mary Aldermanbury was formally opened by the Rt. Hon. the Lord Mayor, Sir Ian Bowater. The handsome granite bust of William Shakespeare, presented in 1896 by Charles Clement Walker of Shropshire, was still standing there for all to read the glowing tribute:

> ... *to the memory of John Heminge and Henry Condell, fellow actors and personal friends of Shakespeare. They lived many years in this parish and are buried here. To their disinterested affection the world owes all that it calls Shakespeare. They alone collected his dramatic writings regardless of pecuniary loss and without the hope of any profit gave them to the world. They thus merited the gratitude of mankind.*

Also appearing on the monument is the following extract from the preface to the First Folio of 1623, addressed by Heminge and Condell to 'the great variety of readers':

Plate I

Memorial in the garden of St. Mary-the-Virgin, Aldermanbury, dedicated in 1896 to Heminge and Condell, Shakespeare's 'fellows', co-actors, friends and business associates. (Alongside stands Mr. F. E. Cleary whose determination to pay tribute to the two men who 'gave us Shakespeare' led to the writing of this book.)

It had bene a thing, we confesse, worthie to have bene wished, that the author himselfe had lived to have set forth, and overseene his owne writings; but since it hath bin ordain'd otherwise, and he by death departed from that right, we pray you do not envie his Friends, the office of their care and paine, to have collected and published them . . . absolute in their numbers as he conceived them who as he was a happie imitator of Nature, was a most gentle expresser of it. His mind and hand went together, and what he thought, he uttered with that easinesse, that we have scarse received from him a blot in his papers.

On the left-hand tablet of the monument is a warm tribute to the two actors who sacrificed so much time and trouble to ensure that the works of Shakespeare did not perish with their author. The simple but sincere account of their self-imposed task should do much to eradicate any misunderstanding of their motives. The inscription reads:

The fame of Shakespeare rests on his incomparable dramas. There is no evidence that he ever intended to publish them and his premature death in 1616 made this the interest of no one else. Heminge and Condell had been co-partners with him in the Globe Theatre, Southwark, and from the accumulated plays there of thirty-five years with great labour selected them. No men then living were so competent having acted with him in them for many years and well knowing his manuscripts. They were published in 1623 in folio thus giving away their private rights therein. What they did was priceless for the whole of his manuscripts with almost all those of the dramas of the period have perished.

The memorial also reproduces the introduction to the 1623 First Folio edition, referring to 'Mr. William Shakespeare's comedies, histories and tragedies published according to the five original copies, London, 1623.' The 'Book' furthermore

7

sets out the editors' simple and touching affirmation, 'We have but collected them [the plays] and done our office to the dead without ambition either of selfe profit or fame, onely to keep the memory of so worthy a friend and fellow alive as was our Shakespeare.'

Before leaving this remarkable memorial, we must confess our regret that the pedestal does not support the bust of John Heminge and Henry Condell. From the Droeshout engraving, the 'Flower' and the 'Chandos' portraits, the Ashbourne and Janssen paintings, the Shakespeare bust in Holy Trinity Church, Stratford-on-Avon, and a few other portraits, (some authentic, some not), we all have a rough idea of the dramatist's physical appearance. What Heminge and Condell looked like we shall, alas, never know.

Contemporary references to Heminge and Condell make it clear that the former was the older man. When the Globe was burnt down in 1613, *A Sonnett upon the pittiful burneing of the Globe playhouse in London* appeared at the time and it furnishes us with a picture of the ageing actor in the following couplet:

> *There with swolne eyes, like druncken Flemminges,*
> *Distressed stood old stuttering Heminges.'*

Furthermore, in his *Masque of Christmas* (1616), Jonson has one of the characters, a deaf dresser called Venus, say, 'Master Burbage has been about and about with me, and so has old Master Hemings too.'

We know neither the date nor place of Heminge's birth, but his father, a gentleman of Worcestershire, hailed from Droitwich, On the other hand, the Shakespearian commentator Malone was of the opinion that Heminges was a Stratford man. It is certain that he lived in the parish of St. Mary Aldermanbury for forty-two years, that he was married there in 1588 to a widow, Rebecca Knell, that of their

fourteen children thirteen were baptised in St. Mary's, and that he himself was buried in St. Mary's churchyard in 1630 under the rose-trees that bloom there to-day.

If his will is anything to go on, Heminge was a 'Citizen and Grocer'. His wife, however, would have looked after the grocery business, leaving Heminge free to pursue his main interests, acting and the theatre. Exactly when he became an actor we cannot definitely say, but there is little doubt that he joined the profession even before Shakespeare did. It would appear, as we have already suggested, that his acting career began with Queen Elizabeth's troupe, moving on with his friend Condell to Lord Strange's Men, (the Privy Council granted this Company a travelling licence on May 6th, 1593, and Heminge's name figures on it), Lord Derby's Servants, and then the Chamberlain's Men, an association that assumed the title of King's Men after James I succeeded Elizabeth in 1603.

As far as Heminge's acting career is concerned, there is ample evidence that he performed in a number of plays by Ben Jonson — *Every Man in his Humour, Every Man out of his Humour, Sejanus, Volpone, The Alchemist* and *Catiline*. Malone's contention that he was the first actor to play the part of Falstaff seems without foundation, although it is easy to see him as Polonius, Kent, Brabantio, Leonato, Capulet and Gonzalo. Among his many other roles, Heminge probably played Julius Caesar and Ross.

It is an interesting conjecture that Henry Condell was Antony to Heminge's Caesar, Malcolm to his Ross, Edgar to his Kent, and Horatio to his Polonius. In the same plays Richard Burbage was undoubtedly Brutus, Macbeth, Lear and Hamlet. One gets the distinct impression that Heminge was usually type-cast. He must have been a reasonably competent actor, but he obviously had a special talent for theatrical administration and accountancy. It is therefore not

surprising to find that he withdrew from acting in or about 1611, in order to devote the whole of his energies to Company affairs. His reputation for efficiency and probity was clearly appreciated by other stage organisations, for there are records of his negotiations with the Master of the Revels on behalf of as many as four companies.[2]

Turning to Henry Condell for a moment, we have already noted that he probably played the part of Ferrex in the 1592 production of *The Seven Deadly Sins*. In *The Organisation and Personnel of the Shakespearian Company,* Baldwin expresses the opinion that between 1598 and 1603 Condell played Benvolio in *Romeo and Juliet,* Don Pedro in *Much Ado about Nothing,* Oliver in *As You Like It,* and Horatio in *Hamlet.* He certainly appeared as the Cardinal in Webster's *Duchess of Malfi.* He was a friendly type, a circumstance reflected in the number of legacies that came his way after the demise of many of his 'fellows'. He was remembered in the wills of such actors as Phillips, Cooke, Tooley, Underwood, and Shakespeare himself. The fact that in three of those wills Condell was named as trustee or executor speaks volumes for his integrity and reliability.

Contemporary records contain a number of references to Henry Condell. A glance at some of them will help to establish his position in Elizabethan society and at the same time will reveal something of his personality. In the first place, although his name usually appears among the top half-dozen in his Company's list of actors, he never achieved the fame of such luminaries as Richard Burbage and Edward Alleyn. He was, nevertheless, a regular performer, playing alongside the great Burbage in most of the dramatic offerings of Beaumont and Fletcher.

Among the information unearthed by patient researchers, the following facts indisputably emerge: Henry Condell became a member of the Wardmote Inquest at St Mary's

Plate II

London street map of 1560 showing Aldermanbury and the corner of Mugle (Monkwell) Street and Silver Street in Cripplegate where Shakespeare lodged with the Mountjoys not far from Heminge and Condell.

Aldermanbury in 1615 and was reappointed in the succeeding year; on March 25th, 1616, he (with Heminge and Burbage) figures in Shakespeare's will, each being left the sum of twenty-six shillings and eightpence; in the same year his name was as high as fourth in the King's Men's list of players in *The Mad Lover,* and a few months later it was second in the cast for *The Knight of Malta;* a year or so afterwards Condell's signature was written in the registers for marriage and baptism in the church of St. Mary's Aldermanbury; in 1618 his name was second in the list of King's Men performing in Fletcher's *The Loyal Subject,* a drama in which Condell played the incompetent flatterer Boroskie; a 1619 entry in the Parish Minute Book of St. Mary's Aldermanbury appoints Condell and Heminge as 'feoffees for our parish land', (a feoffee being a person to whom freehold estate in land is conveyed); possibly in the same year Condell's name headed the list of actors for Fletcher's *The Humorous Lieutenant,* a comedy in which he most likely played Antigonus, King of Syria; then in 1620 he and Heminge were involved in a law suit with John Witter, a ne'er-do-well who married the widow of Augustine Phillips, squandered her captial and went to law to try to obtain her Globe shares.

But the big year in Condell's life was assuredly 1623, the year in which he and Heminge, operating together as editors, brought out the Shakespeare First Folio, an achievement that can never be praised too highly. All lovers of Shakespeare will readily agree with the sentiments expressed in the early seventeetnth century, written in a commonplace book belonging to the Salusbury family:

To yow that joyntly with undaunted paynes
Vowtsafed to chawnte to us thease noble straynes
How mutch yow merrytt by it is not sedd
But yow have pleased the lyving loved the deadd.

Raysede from the woambe of earth a Richer myne
Than Curteys cowlde with all his Castelyne
Assotiatts they dydd but digg for gowlde
But yow for Treasure mutch moare manifold.

Other interesting scraps of information concerning Henry Condell that can be vouched for as authentic refer to his inclusion in 1625 in the list of King's Men, with Condell's name lying second, who were granted an allowance of black cloth for King James's funeral procession; his generous hospitality towards the end of that same year when he entertained a number of his fellow actors in his country house in Fulham; his reply in the year of his death to a complaint in the Chancery Court, lodged against him by Mathew Baldron and his wife, in connection with a dwelling in the Strand, (a property sold a few years later by Mrs. Condell for nearly £1500). Although he was living in Fulham when he died (1627), he was buried in the churchyard of St. Mary's Aldermanbury.

It is only fitting that the St. Mary's Aldermanbury monument to Heminge and Condell bears their simple epitaphs. In Heminge's case the message informs us that 'John Heminge lived in this parish upwards of forty-two years and in which he was married. He had fourteen children, thirteen of whom were baptized, four buried and one married here. October 12, 1630. His wife was also buried here'.

The wording about Condell is almost identical, the only differences being that the younger man lived in the parish for thirty years, had only nine children, (eight of whom were baptized and six buried there), was himself buried in the same churchyard on December 29th, 1627. Singularly appropiate, too, is the quotation from *Henry VIII, Act Three, Scene Two,* which runs:

Let all the ends thou aimst at
Be thy Country's, thy God's and Truth's.

It would appear then that John Heminge and Henry Condell were fairly average men of their time, with no special intellectual or artistic gifts, who had both experienced that indefinable longing to 'strut and fret their hour upon the stage'. The theatre, it would seem, was in their blood. That they should share the desire to tread the boards in various guises ranging from commoner to royal rank is not surprising when we consider the period in which they lived. They had the good fortune to have been born into the richest dramatic era that England had ever known or was likely to know. It was the theatre's golden age — the time of Beaumont and Fletcher, George Chapman, Thomas Decker, John Ford, Robert Greene, Thomas Heywood, Benjamin Jonson, Thomas Kyd, Christopher Marlowe, Philip Massinger, Thomas Middleton, George Peele and John Webster. It was the time of the greatest of them all — William Shakespeare.

II

A thousand poets pried at life,
And only one amid the strife
Rose to be Shakespeare.

Robert Browning.

BEFORE EXAMINING the self-imposed task undertaken by Heminge and Condell, let us consider briefly the man whose work they deemed worthy of preservation. The general opinion would probably be that such a consideration would necessarily be brief in so far as so little is known about William Shakespeare. Indeed, one eighteenth century scholar, George Steevens, sums up the popular view when he says, 'All that is known with any degree of certainty concerning Shakespeare, is — that he was born at Stratford upon Avon, — married and had children there, — went to London, where he commenced actor, and wrote poems and plays, returned to Stratford, made his will, died, and was buried.' After all, his working life, that is to say, the period during which he produced his plays and poems, covered no more than about twenty years.

Many writers about Shakespeare begin by informing their readers that the known facts about the dramatist could be set down on a postcard. Although some of them go on to fill three or four hundred pages about his life and work, they are

16

Mr. WILLIAM

SHAKESPEARES

COMEDIES,
HISTORIES, &
TRAGEDIES.

Published according to the True Originall Copies.

Martin Droeshout sculpsit London.

L O N D O N
Printed by Isaac Iaggard, and Ed. Blount. 1623.

Plate III
Title page of 1623 First Folio.

careful to point out, (more or less following the trail blazed by Steevens), that according to the records, William Shakespeare was baptised on April 26th, 1564; that in the November of 1582 he married Anne Hathaway; that a daughter, Susanna, was christened only six months after the ceremony; that at the beginning of February, 1585, the twins, Hamnet and Judith, were christened; that between 1584 and 1613 he was writing plays and poetry; that he bought New Place in Stratford on May 4th, 1597; that in 1598 he fell foul of the tax collector in St. Helen's parish, London, and was listed as a defaulter; that on February 21st, 1599, he became a lessee/shareholder in land for the Globe theatre; that on October 6th, 1600, he owed thirteen shillings and fourpence in tax in the county of Sussex; that on August 9th, 1608, he and six colleagues leased Blackfriars Theatre for twenty-one years; that towards the end of January, 1616, he drew up his will, revising it on March 25th; that he was buried in Holy Trinity Church, Stratford.

Records also show that during the period 1595 to his death in 1616 he was paid as an actor in a number of plays, (his own and those of other dramatists), was involved in various minor legal suits, bought property both in Stratford and in London, and benefited in the wills of several fellow actors.

His own will was a straightforward document typical of the age in which he lived. Some critics and commentators have tried to read sinister meanings into his bequest to his wife of 'his second best bed', but after all it was the marriage bed and consequently of far more significance to William and Anne than the 'best' bed, which in those days was normally reserved for guests. As Shakespeare's wife, Anne was entitled by law to spend the rest of her life in New Place, looked after by her daughter Susanna. Moreover she had a legal right to a third of her husband's various properties, so she would have been very comfortably off indeed, with or without the bed.

knowledge of foreign places and his detailed allusions to shipwrecks. Unfortunately there is not a scrap of real evidence to support such a neat solution. When the boatswain in *The Tempest* uses expressions like 'yare' or 'take in the topsail' or 'lay her a-hold, a-hold; set her two courses', the nautical language could well have been picked up by Shakespeare from sailors he chatted with in London taverns.

But the true story of William Shakespeare, man of the theatre, has its beginnings in Stratford. By the time he was born the drama had moved a long way from the days of the old miracle and morality plays. The simple booth stage mounted on trestles in the market-place had been superseded by the inn-yard theatre, and both public and private playhouses, (i.e. buildings specifically constructed for the performance of plays), were springing up within the City of London and also outside the walls, particularly south of the river. The popularity of dramatic performances in the capital was clearly demonstrated by the number of theatres built between 1576 and 1614, (during twenty-six years of Shakespeare's lifetime.) The first public playhouse, the Theatre, in Shoreditch was soon competing with the following City theatres: the Curtain, Blackfriars, the Fortune, the Red Bull, Whitefriars, the Phoenix or Cockpit, and Salisbury Court, while south of the Thames were Newington Butts, the Rose, the Swan, the Globe and the Hope. Companies of actors, usually under noble patronage, presented plays, sometimes in London, sometimes in the provinces. There is documentary evidence, admirably assembled by Edgar Fripp, that some of these groups of players visited Stratford.

Between 1569 and 1587 Shakespeare's father, as High Bailiff or Mayor, was undoubtedly responsible for the welfare of such distinguished entertainers as the Queen's Players, the Earl of Worcester's Men, the Earl of Leicester's Men, the Earl of Warwick's Men, Lord Strange's Men, the Countess of

tectum
porticus
orchestra
ingressus
mimorum
ædes
proscænium
planities sive arena

Plate IV
The Swan theatre, London, from a drawing of 1596.

Essex's Men, Earl Derby's Men, Lord Berkeley's Men, Lord Chandos's Men, the Earl of Oxford's Men and the Earl of Stafford's Men. It is reasonable to assume that the young man Shakespeare, thanks to his father's high office, was able to attend some of their performances. It is also more than likely that the significant year for William was 1587 when the Queen's Men were in Stratford. At any rate we know for a fact that later on he was to join that illustrious Company as an actor, a play 'repairer', and subsequently a fully fledged dramatist. There was certainly a vacancy in the Company at that time, for two members of the group quarrelled, fought, and one, William Knell, had been stabbed in the throat and killed.

There can be no certainty, however, that the Queen's Men was the *first* company to which he attached himself. He might just as likely have started with Lord Strange's or Pembroke's Men, for it is on record that he was paid for two acting performances presented before the Queen during the Christmas festivities of 1594. For the first time his name is linked with that of Richard Burbage.

Round about the same time, another threatrical group, Lord Derby's Servants, staged what was probably the initial performance of Shakespeare's *Titus Andronicus*. Two members of the cast were John Heminge and Henry Condell. On the death of their patron, Lord Derby, shortly afterwards, the leading actors transferred to the Lord Chamberlain's Company, thus bringing together three men, (four if we count Richard Burbage), who became firm friends and fellow Thespians and eventually shareholders in the Globe Theatre when it was built in 1599. Naturally, when James I came to the throne in 1603 and placed the Lord Chamberlain's Men under royal patronage, their names appear on the formal patent prepared by the Keeper of the Privy Seal and henceforth they were known as the King's Men. The relevant

25

passage licenses 'these our servants, Lawrence Fletcher, William Shakespeare, Richard Burbage, Augustine Phillips, John Heminges, Henry Condell, William Sly, Robert Armin, Richard Cowley, and the rest of their associates, freely to use and exercise the art and faculty of playing comedies, tragedies, histories, interludes, morals, pastorals, stage-plays and such others, like as they have already studied or hereafter shall use or study, as well for the recreation of our loving subjects as for our solace and pleasure . . .' The wording calls to mind Polonius's comment on the players who visited Elsinore. They are, he says, 'the best actors in the world, either for tragedy, comedy, history, pastoral, pastoral-comical, historical-pastoral, tragical-historical, tragical-comical-historical'.

Before pursuing theatrical matters as they affected William Shakespeare and his 'fellows', we must glance at the dramatist's activites during the 1592/94 period when the London theatres were closed because of the plague. He did not remain idle. At a time when his dramatic outpourings and those of contemporary playwrights counted for little in the field of worthwhile literature, he produced two works that did much for his reputation as a serious writer. He wrote two long narrative poems, both printed by Richard Field, (son of a Stratford tanner who had once had business transactions with Shakespeare's father). They were *Venus and Adonis,* published on April 18th, 1953, and *The Rape of Lucrece* which emerged from the press on May 9th of the following year. It is ironic that these poems, 154 sonnets, two doubtful pieces entitled *The Passionate Pilgrim* and *A Lover's Complaint,* and an enigmatic effort called *The Phoenix and the Turtle* definitely established Shakespeare as a man of letters. His plays (and by then he had written many) counted for very little. Sold for a song, usually to his own Company, they held small interest for the dramatist once they were off the stocks.

The situation then, as far as the King's Men were concerned, was that they had on their books a number of extremely capable actors, headed by the unsurpassable Richard Burbage for whom, it is said, Shakespeare specially created the characters of Hamlet, Othello and Lear. Burbage's only possible rival, indeed, was Edward Alleyn, a great tragic actor who does not appear to have acted in any of Shakespeare's plays.

Another worthy trouper was Robert Armin who perhaps played Feste, Touchstone and — adding a new dimension to fooling — Lear's tragi-comic jester. Other notables were George Bryan, Alexander Cooke (whose theatrical career started as apprentice to Heminge), the low comedian Richard Cowley, Samuel Crosse who excelled in female roles, Nathan Field who probably followed in the footsteps of Shakespeare after his death in 1616, Lawrence Fletcher, Samuel Gilborne (apprentice to Augustine Phillips), William Hughes, William Kempe who almost certainly was the original Dogberry, that huge man John Lowin who may well have played Falstaff, William Ostler, Augustine Phillips, Thomas Pope who was a founder member of the Company, John Rice, Richard Robinson, John Shank, John Sincklo, William Sly, the lightning-quick joker Richard Tarlton (Yorick in *Hamlet*?), Nicholas Tooley and John Underwood.

They had the actors and, thanks largely to William Shakespeare, they had the plays. All they had to decide was where their plays were going to be staged.

Glancing down the list of private theatres that existed in London during Shakespeare's lifetime, we note the Blackfriars Theatre was closed in 1584 and reopened sixteen years later. Near the river in Fleet Street, in or about 1608, stood the Whitefriars Theatre until it was closed in 1629. Not

far away was Salisbury Court which was closed in 1671, while in Drury Lane the Phoenix opened in the year that Shakespeare died and probably closed in 1663. The shortest-lived theatre was Porter's Hall near Ludgate Hill, which opened in 1616 and closed the following year. Among the public theatres were the Globe, the Fortune, the Rose and the Theatre.

In 1599 the Globe Theatre was leased out to shareholders in the Chamberlain's Company. Shakespeare was one, thus becoming entitled to part of the profits and accepting a measure of responsibility for financial outlay. Furthermore he was a 'housekeeper' which meant that part of the building belonged to him. The Burbage brothers, Richard and Cuthbert, owned half of it, while the other half was shared between William Shakespeare, John Heminge, Augustine Phillips, Thomas Pope and Will Kempe. Henry Condell at that time was not a 'sharer' in the Globe, but he acquired an interest during the period 1605/8. It was also in 1608 that a syndicate assumed control of the Blackfriars lease. The annual rent was £40, so each of the seven 'housekeepers' subscribed £5.14s.4d. The new owners were the two Burbages, Shakespeare, Heminge, Condell, Thomas Evans and Sly.

It is not surprising that these actors preferred, if possible, to live near to the area in which they operated. As far as Heminge and Condell were concerned, they both stayed for many years in the parish of St. Mary Aldermanbury; nor could they have selected a more suitable locality. To begin with, they were not only at the hub of the theatrical world; they were also living for a busy period within a stone's throw of the greatest dramatist of all time. They had acted in some of the plays of Ben Jonson. They had pursued the career of the 'upstart crow' with a good deal of interest but, we imagine, few misgivings. They were on intimate terms with the most

eminent of actors, Richard Burbage, and had probably heard that Shakespeare and Burbage were involved in the following scurrilous anecdote, (which may or may not be true). 'Upon a time when Burbage played Richard III there was a citizen grew so far in liking with him that before she went from the play she appointed him to come that night unto her by the name of Richard III. Shakespeare, overhearing their conclusion, went before, was entertained and at his game ere Burbage came. Then message being brought that Richard III was at the door, Shakespeare caused return to be made that William the Conqueror was before Richard III.'

As we have seen, Heminge and Condell had established themselves as actors, playing many parts in what to-day would have been called 'supporting roles'. Shakespeare himself had achieved something of a reputation in his kingly performances. In nearly all theatrical groups there is a fair proportion of type-casting, so we are not surprised to hear Polonius (Heminge) using expressions that could easily have dropped from the lips of Heminge himself. Polonius says:

> . . .Give thy thoughts no tongue,
> Nor any unproportion'd thought his act.
> Be thou familiar, but by no means vulgar.
> Those friends thou hast, and their adoption tried,
> Grapple them to thy soul with hoops of steel;
> But do not dull thy palm with entertainment
> Of each new-hatch'd, unfledg'd comrade. Beware
> Of entrance to a quarrel; but being in
> Bear't that the opposed may beware of thee.
> Give every man thy ear, but few thy voice;
> Take each man's censure, but reserve thy judgment.
> Costly thy habit as thy purse can buy,
> But not express'd in fancy; rich, not gaudy;
> For the apparel oft proclaims the man;

And they in France of the best rank and station
Are of a most select and generous choice in that.
Neither a borrower nor a lender be;
For loan oft loses both itself and friend,
And borrowing dulls the edge of husbandry . . .

It is equally easy to imagine Shakespeare, as the Ghost in the same play, making the audience shudder with his delivery of such lines as:

I could a tale unfold whose lightest word
Would harrow up thy soul, freeze thy young blood,
Make thy two eyes, like stars, start from their spheres,
Thy knotted and combined locks to part,
And each particular hair to stand on end,
Like quills upon the fretful porpentine.

Although it is generally accepted that Heminge actually did play Polonius and Shakespeare the Ghost in *Hamlet*, and although their names (and Condell's) appear on the cast lists of various plays, there are no records of the individual roles they undertook. How dedicated they were to the profession of acting it is difficult to assess. Heminge, and to a lesser degree Condell, seem to have had more interest in theatre management and the business aspects of the playhouse. Shakespeare, deeply committed to providing his Company with plays, simply could not spare the time to develop his talent as an actor. Nevertheless, only someone with an instinctive knowledge of the stage could have written Hamlet's sound advice to the players:

Speak the speech, I pray you, as I pronounc'd it to you, trippingly on the tongue; but if you mouth it, as many of our players do, I had as lief the town-crier spoke my lines. Nor do not saw the air too much with your hand, thus, but use all gently; for in the very torrent, tempest, and, as I may say,

whirlwind of your passion, you must acquire and beget a temperance that may give it smoothness. O, it offends me to the soul to hear a robustious, periwig-pated fellow tear a passion to tatters, to very rags, to split the ears of the groundlings, who, for the most part, are capable of nothing but inexplicable dumb shows and noise. I would have such a fellow whipp'd for o'er-doing Termagant; it out-Herods Herod. Pray you avoid it.

It is quite conceivable that a man who had such an intimate acquaintance with matters theatrical, if he had devoted all his considerable energies to acting, might have out-Burbaged Burbage, As it was, as his contemporary, John Davies the poet from Hereford put it, Shakespeare assuredly 'played some kingly parts in sport'. He also performed lesser roles, expressing his frustration in Sonnet 110 when he said:

Alas, 't is true I have gone here and there
And made myself a motley to the view.

As actors then, Shakespeare, Heminge and Condell were kept well occupied. After three years at the Theatre, (built by James Burbage, Richard's father), during the summer months they appeared at the Globe, a public theatre; in the winter months the Company moved into Blackfriars, a private theatre, They also had many court engagements, performing at Hampton Court, Whitehall and Windsor. When the London theatres were closed — because of the plague or government policy or for any other reason — the King's Men would tour the provinces, visiting such places as Ipswich, Coventry, Marlborough, New Romney, Hythe, Bath and Shrewsbury. In view of the deplorable state of the so-called roads, travelling at that time was a demoralising experience, so possibly because of his writing commitments Shakespeare was excused some of the more villainous journeys.

31

For about four years before the King's Men took over the lease of Blackfriars Theatre, Shakespeare had been living in Silver Street, Cripplegate, presumably in bachelor accommodation. (There is nothing in the records to suggest that his wife ever left Stratford for London.) He stayed in the house of a certain Christopher Mountjoy, a French Huguenot who manufactured ornamental headpieces for ladies. The Mountjoy residence comprised a shop below and living rooms and lodgings above. Standing on the corner formed by Monkwell Street and Silver Street, not far from St. Olave's Church, the dwelling was eminently suitable for Shakespeare. For one thing it was close to St. Paul's Cathedral and the churchyard happened to be the focal point of the book trade. Naturally the well-stocked stalls attracted all sorts of buyers, so Shakespeare had access to a mass of books covering most subjects and at the same time he was in touch with people from all walks of life.

Then again, his lodgings were within a reasonable distance of Blackfriars. He must also have been pleased to have been so near to his two good friends from Aldermanbury, Heminge and Condell. He obviously liked that part of London, for after he retired from the King's Men and returned to Stratford, he bought the Blackfriars Gate-house for £80. It is interesting to note that the property was conveyed in joint ownership to Shakespeare, William Johnson, (host of the Mermaid tavern), John Jackson, ('a gentleman of London'), and none other than John Heminge.

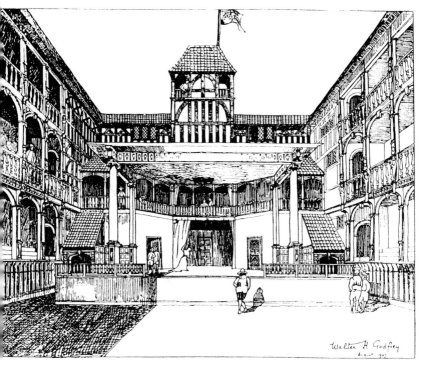

Plate V
Interior of the Fortune Theatre, London. A drawing by Walter H. Godfrey.

III

Yet the work itself shall not be lost for it will ... appear in a new and more beautiful edition.

Benjamin Franklin.

THE PERIOD immediately following Shakespeare's arrival in London was memorable not only for the sudden flowering of English drama; but also because it was rich in momentous historical events. During those golden years the young dramatist would have heard about the Irish Rebellion, the arrest and subsequent execution of the Earl of Essex, Walter Raleigh's imprisonment, the Gunpowder Plot, the colonisation of Virginia, Galileo's astronomical telescope, the discovery of Hudson Bay, the marriage of Pocahontas, and Raleigh's search for El Dorado. It was an age of variety, action and exploration. It was also an age of conflicting opinions about what was right and what was wrong.

Although the theatre was a popular form of entertainment, there were still some who thought it was sinful and believed actors were loose-living, immoral vagabonds. In favour of closing all City playhouses, these narrow-minded Puritans naturally included Blackfriars in their complaints. Their

petition to the City authorities objected to the daily 'resort of people, and such multitudes of coaches (whereof many are Hackney Coaches, bringing people of all sorts) that sometimes all our streetes cannott containe them, but that they clogg upp Ludgate alsoe, in such sort, that both they endanger the one the other, breake downe stalles, throwe downe men's goodes from their shopps. And the inhabitantes there cannott come to their howses, nor bringe in their necessary provisions of beere, wood, coale or haye, nor the Tradesmen or shopkeepers utter their wares, nor the passenger goe to the comon water staires without danger of their lives and lymmes, wherebye alsoe many times, quarrelles and effusion of blood hath followed; and what further danger may be occacŏned by the broyles plottes or practises of such an unrulie multitude of people yff they should gett head, yor wisedomes cann conceave; theise inconveniencies fallinge out almost everie daie in the winter tyme (not forbearinge the tyme of Lent) from one or twoe of the clock till sixe att night, which beinge the tyme alsoe most usuall for christeninges and burialls and afternoones service, wee cannott have passage to the Church for the performance of those necessary duties, the ordinary passage for a great part of the precinct aforesaid beinge close by the playhouse dore.'

Despite the detailed nature and good measure of truth of the petition, it had no effect whatsoever. The play-loving monarch simply gave the King's Men another licence granting them permission to play in their two usual houses, the Globe in Surrey and Blackfriars in the City of London. The names appearing on the new licence were those of John Heminge, Richard Burbage, Henry Condell, John Lowin, Nicholas Tooley, John Underwood, Nathan Field, Robert Benfield, Robert Gough, William Ecclestone, Richard Robinson and John Shank. Shakespeare had died two years previously, and so his name does not figure on the document.

Shakespeare's death in 1616 was of course a cruel blow to the King's Men, but it was by no means an irreparable loss. After all, the Company still had his plays and there were plenty of them. There would be no more new Shakespearian masterpieces to pack the theatres, but they could revive the best of what they had and there were other dramatists. As an actor, too, William was replaceable. His three greatest friends, Heminge, Condell and Richard Burbage, no doubt mourned longer than the rest of his 'fellows', but even for them time was the inevitable healer.

A heavier blow, however, was to fall on the King's Men in 1619 when the company's principal actor, Richard Burbage, died and with him went Macbeth, Hamlet, Othello, Lear and a whole host of stage characters. He was mourned by a friend in the following funeral elegy:

He's gone, and with him what a world is dead!
Which he revived, to be revived so
No more! Young Hamlet, Old Hieronimo,
King Lear, the grieved Moor, and more beside
That lived in him have now for ever died.
Oft have I seen him leap into the grave,
Suiting the person, that he seemd to have
Of a sad lover, with so true an eye
That then I would have sworn he meant to die ——
Oft have I seen him play this part in jest
So lively that spectators, and the rest
Of his sad crew, whilst he but seemed to bleed,
Amazed thought even that he died indeed!

Where could the King's Men find a player of such astonishing versatility? Could there ever be another Richard Burbage? His only possible rival was Edward Alleyn, but he was fully committed as head of the Lord Admiral's Company.

It was during this period that Heminge and Condell

undertook the tremendous task of editing and publishing an 'omnibus' edition of Shakespeare's plays. They must have discussed the project with the playwright before his death and it is just as reasonable to suppose that they also sought the help and advice of Richard Burbage. Shakespeare, though obviously well aware of the value of his work, may not have been as interested in the venture as might have been expected. It may well have been his intention to revise his plays himself and offer them to the general public. It would have been better so, but death claimed him before his plans bore fruit.

It must be remembered that Heminge and Condell had already seen an indifferent and dishonest collection of what purported to be Shakespeare's plays brought out by the publisher, William Jaggard, in 1619. The same man was also responsible for the publication of a slim volume of verse, *The Passionate Pilgrim,* again with Shakespeare's name on the title page, although only five of the poems were his. Burbage's death left Heminge and Condell as the two senior members of what had come to be looked upon as Shakespeare's own Company. To avoid further piracies, and to keep their friend's memory green, it is not surprising that they decided to assemble all of Shakespeare's dramatic offerings, edit them carefully and publish them in one definitive folio volume.

They must been influenced, moreover, by the publication, in the year of Shakespeare's death, of Ben Jonson's *Works,* meticulously prepared in folio, an up-to-date compilation of the dramatist's writings up to 1616.

With regard to this volume, it is worth noting that in his list of 'principall Comoedians' in *Every Man in his Humour,* Jonson puts Shakespeare's name first. (It is possible he played the elder Knowell.) Shakespeare did not appear in *Every Man out of his Humour,* but in Jonson's list of 'principall Tragoedians' in *Sejanus,* Shakespeare again rates highly.

Plate VI
Ben Jonson.

Many believe that Shakespeare was responsible for Jonson's introduction to the Chamberlain's Men. According to Nicholas Rowe, 'his acquaintance with Ben Jonson began with a remarkable piece of Humanity and good Nature; Mr. Jonson, who was at that time altogether unknown to the World, had offer'd one of his Plays to the Players, in order to have it Acted; and the persons into whose Hands it was put, after having turn'd it carelessly and superciliously over, were just upon returning it to him with an ill-natured Answer, that it would be of no service to their Company, when Shakespeare luckily cast his Eye upon it, and found something so well in it as to engage him first to read it through, and afterwards to recommend Mr. Jonson and his Writings to the Publick. After this they were profess'd friends'.

If the publication of Jonson's *Works* helped stimulate Heminge and Condell into doing something about their friend's plays, then Shakespeare's kind gesture was amply rewarded. They must, at any rate, have said to themselves that if any plays deserved preserving for posterity, those of William Shakespeare should take priority.

It was a brave undertaking and a risky one. As the two editors said in their dedication to the volume they produced, 'We are fallen upon the ill fortune to mingle two of the most diverse things that can be, fear and rashness; rashness in the enterprise and fear in the success'. The immensity of their task would have daunted men less devoted than John Heminge and Henry Condell.

At the time they went to work on the First Folio, Shakespeare had penned thirty-six plays, (thirty-seven if we include *Pericles* which is believed to be not entirely his). Determined to eliminate any 'stolen and surreptitious copies, maimed and deformed by the frauds and stealths of injurious imposters', the enthusiastic editors tackled the many

41

problems they encountered ruthlessly and without compromise. They had been friends of Shakespeare for many years; they had acted with him in his own plays and in those of his fellow dramatists; they had attended rehearsals with him and seen his quick mind at work. They were ideally qualified to decide which lines had the authentic Shakespearian ring and which had not. If Shakespeare could have chosen his own editors, he would assuredly have selected Heminge and Condell.

But before examining their editorial commitment in closer detail, we would do well to define two or three essential terms of reference. To begin with, nineteen plays had already appeared before the publication of the 1623 First Folio. They had been published in quarto editions, i.e. on paper where a sheet is doubly folded to produce four leaves or eight pages, and some of these Quartos, notably *Romeo and Juliet, The Merry Wives of Windsor, Henry V* and *Hamlet,* are of inferior quality. Sometimes the meaning is obscure, speeches are mixed up, word order is confused, unwarranted alterations to the text occur. On the other hand, some of the 'good' Quartos are superior to the Folio versions.

If a book is printed in folio, a larger size of paper is used, ranging from eleven to sixteen inches in length and from eight to eleven inches in width. (The printing of Shakespeare's First Folio in 1623 ran to roughly a thousand copies selling at a pound each or, in to-day's values, about thirty pounds.)

The 'book' in terms of Elizabethan playhouse was simply the prompt copy or the acting version of the dramatist's text. It was the Book-keeper's job to have it censored by the Master of the Revels. This official and his assistants were responsible for organising court entertainments, keeping in touch with the various acting groups, providing them with props and costumes, and seeing that the actors were properly paid.

Finally, when texts are described as 'parallel', it means that there is not a great deal of difference between the Quarto and Folio versions. This has come about because, of the eighteen plays in the First Folio never before published, fourteen were based on 'good' Quartos which they followed very closely.

The initial moves in the production of the First Folio are regrettably not recorded. The original idea might very well have come from Shakespeare himself in the year of his death. The notion of a collection of all his plays might have appealed to him and he might have brought up the subject in casual conversation with his good friends and companions, Heminge and Condell. On the other hand, if the conception of an 'omnibus' volume emanated from Heminge and Condell, (after hearing of the Jonson project), they must have discussed the scheme with Shakespeare and probably with Richard Burbage. Nor must one rule out the possibility of a small group of publishers/stationers getting together in what promised to be a lucrative venture and then approaching Heminge and Condell to ask if they would act as editors. That there was a demand for printed plays is evident from the fact that at least twenty publishers had thought it fit to bring out various editions of single plays by Shakespeare between 1594 and 1619. Alternatively Heminge and Condell may have made the first move, seeking the publishing syndicate's co-operation.

One thing is certain. Heminge and Condell had undertaken a mammoth task. The rough material they had to work on comprised old prompt books that had long been collecting dust in the theatres themselves; quarto editions already printed, some of which were in a deplorable condition; copies that had been made of Shakespeare's own manuscripts; the author's 'foul papers', (rough drafts sufficiently coherent to serve as a scenario but not yet up to the standard of a prompt-book); 'assembled' texts or copies put together from

actors' memorised parts. The editors did, indeed, have a great deal to contend with, and though we may not entirely agree with the comments of Doctor Johnson, we are forced to admit that there is a fair measure of truth in his words when he observes that:

> *To have a text corrupt in many places, and in many doubtful, is, among the authours that have written since the use of types, almost peculiar to Shakespeare. Most writers, by publishing their own works, prevent all various readings, and preclude all conjectural criticism . . . But of the works of Shakespeare the condition has been far different: he sold them, not to be printed, but to be played. They were immediately copied for the actors, and multiplied by transcript after transcript, vitiated by the blunders of the penman, or changed by the affectation of the player; perhaps enlarged to introduce a jest, or mutilated to shorten the representation; and printed at last without the concurrence of the authour, without the consent of the proprietor, from compilations made by chance or by stealth out of the separate parts written for the theatre; and thus thrust into the world surreptitiously and hastily, they suffered another deprivation from the ignorance and negligence of the printers, as every man who knows the state of the press in that age will readily conceive.*

It may be safely assumed that Heminge and Condell set out to present their readers with the most authoritative text possible. If there were several versions available, they bound themselves to select the one that came nearest to the dramatist's original intention. The more carefully we examine the results of their labours in the First Folio, the more clearly we can see that at no stage in their editorship were they content to take the easy way out. When they were dealing with unreliable and possibly pirated texts containing passages

that, according to their knowledge of the man, Shakespeare could never have written, they searched indefatigably for other sources and would not rest until they could produce what they considered to be the genuine Shakespeare. They had worked shoulder to shoulder with the dramatist for so many years that they could never mistake his characteristic style. Their judgment could be safely backed. They knew that he had an unrivalled command over words, an unflagging inventiveness and a strange facility for getting things right at the first attempt. Crossings-out and corrections were rare. If Heminge and Condell could not recognise the work of the 'Master', nobody could.

Nobody could deny that the most suitable editors for Shakespeare's plays at that particular time were his two 'fellows', Heminge and Condell. What has surprised many commentators is that the notorious William Jaggard was allowed to be a member of the publishing team. Quite overlooking his cavalier treatment of *The Passionate Pilgrim*, we cannot ignore Jaggard's involvement, already mentioned, with the publication of a number of plays he attributed to Shakespeare. The plays in question were:

A Midsummer Night's Dream
The Merchant of Venice
Sir John Oldcastle
Henry the Fifth
King Lear
The Merry Wives of Windsor
A Yorkshire Tragedy
Pericles Prince of Tyre
York and Lancaster (in two parts)

Because six of the plays were printed for T.P. or Thomas Pavier, the work is usually referred to as 'the Pavier Shakespeare'. It was no doubt intended to compete with Ben Jonson's *Works*.

Not only were half-a-dozen of the plays wrongly dated; three of them — *Sir John Oldcastle, A Yorkshire Tragedy* and probably *Pericles Prince of Tyre* — were not the work of Shakespeare. Two others — *Henry the Fifth* and *The Merry Wives of Windsor* — were full of inaccuracies. Jaggard's duplicity must have so infuriated the King's Men that they lodged an official complaint with the Lord Chamberlain, and he in turn got in touch with the Stationers' Company, whose court ruling was that henceforth no plays in the King's Men's repertoire would be printed without their approval.[3] Frightened off by the manner in which events were shaping, Jaggard persuaded Pavier to abandon the project.

Although Shakespeare himself and the rest of the King's Men had been scurvily treated by William Jaggard, it must be borne in mind that *The Passionate Pilgrim* irregularity had occurred as far back as 1598 or 1599 and had probably been forgotten by 1619. As for the Shakespeare collection (so-called) of 1619, Jaggard could have accused Thomas Pavier as the instigator of the literary fraud, saying that he himself had done no more than print the plays on Pavier's behalf. In any event the ten plays were never issued in one volume, but were printed as individual quartos to be sold separately.

For whatever reason Jaggard's past misdemeanours were overlooked and he became one of the consortium appointed to publish the 1623 First Folio. The other members of the team, all belonging to the Stationers' Company, were Edward Blount, John Smethwick, William Aspley, and Jaggard's son Isaac who, after his father's death in 1623, took over the management of the firm. Blount held the rights of *Pericles* and *Antony and Cleopatra;* Smethwick owned the rights of *The Taming of the Shrew, Romeo and Juliet, Love's Labour's Lost* and *Hamlet;* Aspley's holdings were *Henry IV Part Two* and *Much Ado about Nothing;* William Jaggard could

possibly have claimed *Troilus and Cressida,* but he had also printed the seven Shakespeare plays (counting *Pericles*) owned by Pavier.

In any case, William Jaggard alone was not the moving spirit behind the First Folio enterprise. After all, the imprint on the title-page quotes *Isaac* Jaggard and Edward Blount as the printers, whereas the colophon clearly states that the cost of the project was borne by 'W. Jaggard, Ed. Blount, I Smithweeke and W. Aspley'.

If these four agreed to pool their resources in order to publish Shakespeare's plays in one large volume, it can be safely assumed that they believed themselves to be on a worthwhile proposition. With them the profit motive weighed very heavily. With the two editors, Heminge and Condell, pecuniary advantage played hardly any part. Their sole purpose was to give the world true versions of Shakespeare's plays, keeping as close as possible to the original creations of the playwright. The magnitude of the task they undertook and the extent to which their endeavours were successful can best be appreciated by examining the plays individually as they were presented in the Shakespeare First Folio. We shall try to get at the facts, but in a world where information cannot all be verified, a certain amount of conjecture and speculation is inevitable.

IV

Shakespeare's rich and varied lore.

Sir Walter Scott

O F THE thirty-six plays (*Pericles* was not included) published in the 1623 First Folio, eighteen were appearing in printed form for the first time. In the case of five of these, Heminge and Condell produced their Folio texts from transcripts prepared by Ralph Crane who served the King's Men in the capacity of scribe or scrivener. The five plays in question were *The Two Gentlemen of Verona, The Merry Wives of Windsor, Measure for Measure, The Winter's Tale* and *The Tempest.* The first two were probably copied from the theatre prompt-book, while for the other three the two editors most likely relied on 'foul' papers.

For the seven following plays Heminge and Condell utilised 'foul' papers as their guides: *Comedy of Errors, The Taming of the Shrew, All's Well that Ends Well, Antony and Cleopatra, Coriolanus, Timon of Athens* and *Henry VIII.* For four more — *Julius Caesar, As You Like It, Macbeth* and *Cymbeline* — the editors made use of prompt-books or transcripts of them. For *Henry VI Part One* they were indebted to the author's manuscript. As for *King John,* they had at their disposal the author's copy that had served the Company as a prompt-book.

48

Of the plays that remain, Heminge and Condell must have had access to fairly reliable quarto editions of a further fourteen — *Much Ado About Nothing,* where the Folio version very closely follows the Quarto of 1600; *Love's Labour's Lost; A Midsummer Night's Dream; The Merchant of Venice; Richard II; Titus Andronicus; Romeo and Juliet; Hamlet; King Lear; Othello; Henry IV Part One; Henry IV Part Two; Troilus and Cressida; Richard III.*

The Quarto edition of *Much Ado About Nothing* was exceptionally clear and presented Heminge and Condell with very few snags. Hardly any changes were required in the translation of Quarto to Folio text; alterations in stage directions were minimal. The theory that the copy of the Quarto they used had been used as a prompt-book no longer attracts the commentators. When Heminge and Condell handed over their copy of the Quarto version to the printers, it is possible that they also provided a manuscript prompt-book. A close study of the stage directions and the designation of characters is richly revealing.

In the case of *Love's Labour's Lost,* all the evidence suggests that the Quarto was based on 'foul' papers. Nowadays it has been accepted that there had been a 'bad' quarto, but it had been lost. Heminge and Condell based their Folio version on the 'good' Quarto of 1598, the Quarto that ends with the cryptic finale:

The words of Mercurie
Are harsh after the songs of Apollo:
You that way; we this way.

The first Quarto edition of *A Midsummer Night's Dream* was published in 1600, but a reprint came out in 1619 and it was this later Quarto that supplied Heminge and Condell with their material for the Folio version. Dover Wilson insists, probably correctly, that the editors made use of the

prompt-book alongside the Second Quarto. When he says that the First Quarto was printed from a theatrical prompt-book, it is less easy to accept his opinion.

First printed in 1600, the Quarto edition of *The Merchant of Venice* was also reprinted in 1619, but it was on the First Quarto that Heminge and Condell drew for their Folio version. It may well be, as Dover Wilson points out, that this First Quarto had seen service in the theatre as a prompt-book.

We know of five quarto editions of that very popular play, *Richard II,* the first of which was most probably based on 'foul' papers. There has been a good deal of argument concerning which quarto Heminge and Condell relied on when they were preparing their Folio version. All the evidence indicates that a later Quarto (the Fifth) was used, except for the abdication scene which is more likely to have emanated from the prompt-book or some other authentic manuscript.

The early history of *Titus Andronicus* is admittedly obscure. The First Quarto edition of the play appeared in 1594, but it was badly damaged and a second quarto had to be put together in 1600, copied from its predecessor but with several conjectural insertions. This Second Quarto was reprinted in 1611 and it was from this Third Quarto that the 1623 Folio version was prepared. Heminge and Condell also had recourse to some other authority in order to carry out a minor textual reconstruction. They did not resort to the prompt-book, but simply introduced a manuscript extract, possibly from the Second Quarto.

From a textual point of view, the history of *Romeo and Juliet* closely resembles that of *Love's Labours Lost.* In each case a 'bad' quarto was superseded by a 'good' one and neither was entered in the Stationers' Register. The 'good' quartos were printed for the same man, Cuthbert Burby. In 1609 the 'good' quarto of *Romeo and Juliet* was reprinted and

it was from that version that Heminge and Condell built up the Folio version. It seems fairly certain that this Second Quarto never saw service as a prompt-book, and wherever there were changes in the stage directions, they were carried out in the printing-house.

The textual history of *Hamlet* is long and complicated, beginning with a play of that name which was presented in 1594 at Newington Butts. Possibly written by Thomas Kyd, this play was the basis of Shakespeare's tragedy which emerged in quarto form in 1603, (assembled from the actors' remembered lines and considerably shorter than the full version). Then followed a second quarto version in 1604/5. The title-page reads, 'The Tragicall Historie of Hamlet, Prince of Denmarke. By William Shakespeare. Newly imprinted and enlarged to almost as much againe as it was, according to the true and perfect coppie.' The compositor was obviously incompetent and probably in a hurry, for the Second Quarto contains a mass of mistakes of all kinds. He was also an indifferent speller. Nevertheless, according to several commentators, Heminge and Condell based their Folio version on an altered and corrected copy of the Second Quarto.

When preparing *King Lear* for press, Heminge and Condell clearly depended on the 1608 Quarto version, a text generally regarded as unsatisfactory and one containing a number of unintelligible passages. E.K. Chambers suggests that the Quarto copy stems from a reported text 'produced by shorthand and not memorisation'. Alice Walker's ingenious theory is that the contaminated portions of the text spring from a careless scribe writing from dictation, (probably one boy actor dictating to another — Goneril to Regan, for example, who would especially recollect their own parts in the play). Examining the problem from all angles, we can only conclude that the two editors based their Folio version on the

Quarto edition as collated by and corrected by a manuscript, most likely the prompt-book.

The latest of the Shakespeare quartos was that of *Othello* which was published in 1622, obviously with the sanction of the King's Men. This particular version seems to have been printed from a transcript prepared in 1620. Ten years later a second quarto was printed from the first, a version that had obviously been influenced in parts by the Folio edition of Heminge and Condell. A good case has been drawn up by Alice Walker that the Folio was dependent on a doctored copy of the Quarto. There are indeed so many possibilities that it is difficult to arrive at a completely satisfying conclusion. The most convincing solution is that a careless scribe prepared a transcript (from 'foul' papers) and from it emerged the 1622 Quarto. Heminge and Condell produced their Folio version from this text, but they insisted on collating it with the prompt-book.

Opinions seem to be divided about the first part of *Henry IV*. We know that the First Quarto was published in 1598 and that Falstaff used to be Oldcastle, (more or less vouched for in the epilogue to the second part of the play). Heminge and Condell prepared their Folio version from the 1613 text of the Fifth Quarto and there is no evidence that they resorted to the prompt-book.

Two years later appeared the Quarto edition of *Henry IV Part Two*, on which Heminge and Condell relied for their Folio version. The editors also had no hesitation in referring to the prompt-book, a recourse that is supported by the large amount of revision and restoration, but at the same time they did not print directly from it. As with *Part One*, the second part is divided into acts and scenes. Unlike *Part One*, the second part has been noticeably pruned of colloquialisms, a strong indication that a literary reviser has been at work. M.A. Shaaber, who brought out a new *Variorum Shakespeare*

in 1940, believes that Heminge and Condell copied from a manuscript by the ubiquitous Crane. Alice Walker argues firmly that they relied on a modified reprint of the Quarto. Each makes out a persuasive case, but only one or the other can be right — or, of course, neither.

One of the most baffling plays in the Folio from the textual angle is indubitably *Troilus and Cressida*. To begin with, the play was entered twice in the Stationers' Register, first of all in 1603 for James Roberts, and secondly in 1609 for two young stationers, Richard Bonian and Henry Walley. Roberts was convinced that the play had been acted; Bonian and Walley were of the opinion that it had not. Later in 1609 the two stationers brought out a quarto edition. When Heminge and Condell came to deal with their Folio version, *Troilus and Cressida* was intended to follow *Romeo and Juliet* as a tragedy, but in 1623 Walley would not give Jaggard permission to reprint his copy. Jaggard had started work on *Troilus and Cressida,* but in view of the situation he was forced to abandon it, leaving what he considered to be ample space to accommodate the rest of the play if there should be a change of circumstances. Subsequently despairing of getting permission to print *Troilus and Cressida,* he proposed to put in its place *Timon of Athens* (which was too short to fill the space available). Then Walley suddenly changed his mind and allowed the Folio printers to go ahead as originally planned. Heminge and Condell then presented a version based largely on the 1609 Quarto, modified here and there by reference to a manuscript. Had matters proceeded without a hitch, no doubt the Folio version would have differed very little from the Quarto rendering.

Anyway, Heminge and Condell eventually disposed of the play in a sort of indeterminate region somewhere between the Histories and the Tragedies. It is, indeed, a puzzling play, full of pitfalls for the unwary and problems for the student. One

point on which the commentators *do* tend to agree is that the Quarto readings are by and large superior to those of the Folio.

The reverse can be said in the case of *Richard the Third,* where there is a wide divergence between Folio and Quarto, with the former offering indisputably the better text. In *The Textual History of 'Richard III'* by David Lyall Patrick, the author maintains that the Quarto was produced from a reported version of the play, a rendering put together by the members of the Company under the direction of the book-keeper during a provincial tour. Heminge and Condell mainly copied the Sixth Quarto of 1622, modified by an authoritative manuscript which was more likely to have been a set of 'foul' papers than a prompt-book.

That leaves us with four more plays, (always setting aside *Pericles,* which was rejected by Heminge and Condell as non-Shakespearian). These four are *Twelfth Night, Henry V* and parts two and three of *Henry VI.*

The editors of the 1623 Folio might very well have wished that the rest of Shakespeare's plays had presented as few problems as *Twelfth Night.* For once such eminent commentators as Dover Wilson and E.K. Chambers are in full agreement concerning the source of the Folio version. As with *Julius Caesar, As You Like It, Macbeth* and *Cymbeline,* the editors worked from a prompt-book or a copy of one. From that same prompt-book the actors in *Twelfth Night* were prompted when the play was presented at the Middle Temple on February 2nd, 1602.

Queen Elizabeth I was in attendance and the occasion was described by a law student, John Manningham, in the following terms in his diary: 'At our feast wee had a play called Twelve night or what you will . . . A good practise in it to make the steward believe his lady widdowe was in Love with him by counterfayting a lettre, as from his Lady in

generall termes, telling him what shee liked best in him, and prescribing his gesture in smiling, his apparaile etc. And then when he came to practise making him beleeve they took him to be heady'. Obviously *Twelfth Night* enjoyed a good measure of popularity. It is curious, therefore, that it never appeared in quarto. On the other hand, it is fortunate that Heminge and Condell had access to such a clear straightforward text as the prompt-book.

As for *Henry V,* although three quarto versions were published, (including the 'bad' Quarto of 1600), Heminge and Condell did not turn to any of them as a basis for their Folio version. The general concensus of opinion supports the belief that the Quarto is a reported text with more than one actor supplying the lines. Not only that. The play as presented in the Quarto has undergone considerable abridgement, (possibly for staging in the provinces). It is not surprising then that the two editors made use of Shakespeare's 'foul' papers, as Dover Wilson recognised. Various contradictions, misnumbering of lines, insertions, typically Shakespearian spellings, misprints, confusion of characters and omissions all combine to rule out any suggestion of the prompt-book being used.

We are now left with parts two and three of *Henry VI,* both of which, oddly enough, were written before part one. First appearing in quarto (1594) and octavo (1595), they became known as 'The Contention between the Houses of York and Lancaster'. The quarto edition had on its title-page: 'The first part of the contention betwixt the two famous Houses of Yorke and Lancaster . . . with the notable Rebellion of Jacke Cade: and the Duke of Yorke's first claime unto the Crowne'. The title-page of the octavo volume read: 'The true Tragedie of Richard Duke of Yorke, and the death of good King Henrie the Sixt, with the whole contention betweene the two Houses Lancaster and Yorke, as it was sundrie times acted by

the Right Honourable the Earle of Pembrooke his Servants'.

Both versions were reprinted twice, (in 1600 and 1619), perhaps from editions corrected by somebody with only a hazy recollection of a theatrical presentation. As with *Henry VI Part One*, Heminge and Condell made their Folio copies from the author's fair copy on which would be scribbled notes by the book-keeper and which had been employed by the prompter. It was not until the two parts of the Contention became the property of the Lord Chamberlain's Company that they were associated with *Part One* to form a trilogy. Whatever manuscript served the editors as a basis for their Folio texts, it must at some time have furnished the players with a prompt-book.

On the whole, one is inclined to go along with W.W. Greg when he says that 'the most reasonable supposition seems to be that authorial fair copy, which still left something to be desired, was in the first instance used by the prompter with a minimum of editing for the stage, that after the manuscript reached the Chamberlain's Men it was worked over and partly rewritten, that a new prompt-copy was prepared, and the old manuscript handed to the printer. Of the new prompt-book we know nothing: we may suppose that in its preparation errors and confusions of the original were corrected, but this, it must be admitted, is rather a pious belief than a confident conviction'.

V

There must be a man behind the book.

R. W. Emerson

HEMINGE AND CONDELL, then, (two actors who had never before carried out the unenviable labours of editorship), had taken upon themselves the task of producing in one volume an 'omnibus' edition of all the plays of William Shakespeare. They were already fairly well occupied with the stage presentations of Shakespeare's Company, both as players and as administrators, yet they somehow found time to collect and edit the works of the greatest dramatist the world has ever known, retaining all that was good and rejecting all that was inferior in their indefatigable efforts to give posterity the real Shakespeare.

If we look at the Alexander text of the complete works of William Shakespeare, we find that thirty-seven plays are included. This apparent discrepancy arises because Professor Alexander decided that in spite of divided opinions concerning *Pericles*, the play contained enough material that was essentially Shakespearian to justify its appearance alongside the other texts.

In the preamble to the actual plays in the 1623 Folio is printed 'A Catalogue of the severall Comedies, Histories, and Tragedies contained in this volume'.

Comedies.

The Tempest
The Two Gentlemen of Verona
The Merry Wives of Windsor
Measure for Measure
The Comedy of Errours
Much adoo about Nothing
Loves Labour lost
Midsommer Nights Dreame
The Merchant of Venice
As you Like it
The Taming of the Shrew
All is well, that Ends well
Twelfe-Night, or what you will
The Winters Tale

Histories.

The Life and Death of King John
The Life and Death of Richard the second
The First part of King Henry the fourth
The Second part of K. Henry the fourth
The Life of King Henry the Fift
The First part of King Henry the Sixt
The Second part of King Hen. The Sixt
The Third part of King Henry the Sixt
The Life & Death of Richard the Third
The Life of King Henry the Eight

Tragedies.

The Tragedy of Coriolanus
Titus Andronicus
Romeo and Juliet
Timon of Athens
The Life and death of Julius Ceasar
The Tragedy of Macbeth
The Tragedy of Hamlet

King Lear
Othello, the Moore of Venice
Anthony and Cleopater
Cymbeline King of Britaine

It also states on the title-page that the plays have been 'truely set forth, according to their first originall', presumably a phrase used by Jaggard to present the claim that the texts had emanated from authoritative sources, i.e. versions of the plays as they had been staged in the theatres — full texts not necessarily containing everything the author had written.

Then follow the names of 'the principall actors in all these playes', headed, as might have been expected, by William Shakespeare, Richard Burbage and John Heminge. Henry Condell is the eighth name on the list.

Also figuring among the preliminary matter are a poem addressed to the reader; a dedication to William, Earl of Pembroke, and Philip, Earl of Montgomery; an epistle addressed to 'the great variety of readers'; and finally a number of prefatory verses, including a lengthy eulogy in praise of Shakespeare from the pen of Ben Jonson, a sonnet by Hugh Holland 'Upon the lines and life of the famous scenicke poet, Master William Shakespeare', and two other poems to Shakespeare's memory — one by L. Digges, who in his youth had been a near neighbour of Shakespeare, Heminge and Condell in the parish of St. Mary Aldermanbury, and the other by 'I.M.' (possibly James Mabbe of Oxford University).

The Jonson poem is too long to quote in full, but the following lines will indicate how highly esteemed Shakespeare was by a rival dramatist:

Soule of the Age!
The applause! delight! the wonder of our Stage!
My Shakespeare, rise; I will not lodge thee by

Chaucer, or Spenser, or bid Beaumont lye
A little further, to make thee a roome:
Thou art a Moniment, without a tombe,
And art alive still, while thy Booke doth live,
And we have wits to read, and praise to give.

Holland, a University man from Cambridge extols Shakespeare as the man that —

...made the dainty Playes,
Which made the Globe of heav'n and earth to ring.

Leonard Digges, whose eulogy includes a reference to Shakespeare's monument at Stratford, had evidently attended such plays as *Romeo and Juliet* and *Julius Caesar* and had found them far more pleasing than Ben Jonson's tragedies, *Sejanus* and *Catiline*.

Mabbe's laudatory poem is short but none the less sincere and can be quoted in full:

Wee wondred Shakespeare that thou went'st so soone
From the world's stage, to the Grave's Tyring-roome.
Wee thought thee dead, but this thy printed worth,
Tels thy Spectators, that thou went'st but forth
To enter with applause. An Actor's Art,
Can dye, and live, to acte a second part.
That's but an Exit *of Mortalitie;*
This, a Re-entrance to a Plaudite.

A number of readers may find the wording of the dedicatory epistle to the Earl of Pembroke and the Earl of Montgomery somewhat subservient and obsequious, but they must take into consideration the fact that in those days patronage was the rule rather than the exception, and for a writer to seek the backing of a wealthy member of the nobility was entirely acceptable. Many patrons were not averse to

basking in their protégés' adulation; some had a genuine desire to sponsor the arts. From a writer's point of view, the financial support of a rich notability was always welcome and in lots of cases essential. Without it, indeed, some authors could never have managed.

The drama, too, had its patrons and in that respect William Shakespeare was more fortunate than most. His two long poems, *Venus and Adonis* and *The Rape of Lucrece*, enjoyed the patronage of the Earl of Southampton; his sonnet sequence was possibly patronised by the same noble lord; the company of actors to which he belonged was sponsored by the Lord Chamberlain and, later, by the King; and although Shakespeare died before the volume appeared, his dramatic works were patronised by the sons of Henry Herbert, Earl of Pembroke.

Not only was it normal procedure for writers to dedicate their artistic productions to their patrons; it was also to be expected that such dedications tended to lapse into fulsome and flowery expressions that to-day might be condemned as grovelling. Heminge and Condell, therefore, were only showing proper respect when they referred to 'an incomparable paire of brethren', the 'humble offer of his [Shakespeare's] plays', their two patrons descending 'to the reading of these trifles'.

More interesting than the flattery is the Editors' assurance that they had merely collected the plays 'to procure his [Shakespeare's] Orphanes Guardians'. Their sincerity also emerges when they say that Shakespeare did not have 'the fate, common with some, to be exequutor to his owne writings'.

Their appeal to 'the great variety of readers' is particularly touching, especially when they recommend the purchase of their book — 'Judge your six-pen'orth, your shillings worth, your five shillings worth at a time, or higher, so you rise to the

just rates, and welcome. But whatever you do, Buy.' Even more significant are their comments on sundry stolen or pirated copies of the plays, and their guarantee that these disreputable versions 'are now offer'd to your view cur'd, and perfect of their limbes'.

For some idea of the dramatist's physical appearance we turn again to the portrait of Shakespeare, the copper-plate engraving by Martin Droeshout that is presented on the title-page of the First Folio. Far from finding universal favour, the Droeshout portrait has been described as having 'little technical merit', 'obviously the attempt of a novice', a 'pudding-faced effigy', and yet the same likeness could be described by A. L. Rowse in the following terms: ' . . . the arched eyebrows, the large fine eyes that we can see would easily be capable of a wide range of expression, full of intelligence. The nose is large and rather sensual, yet with sensibility indicated in the flare of the nostril — and we know that he had an acute sense of smell. The mouth small and well-formed, with a suggestively feminine curve of the lips, almost a Cupid's bow. The well-rounded cheeks suggest the mobile face of an actor, with easy changes of expression; the face rather hairless, with light moustache and little tuft beneath the lower lip, the hair worn long. What a powerful expression it gives: that searching look of the eyes understanding everything, what a forehead, what a brain!'

Ben Jonson, who knew Shakespeare well, also found the Droeshout portrait a satisfactory likeness. His views are felicitously expressed in his poem addressed 'To the reader' (of the First Folio):

This figure, that thou here seest put,
 It was for gentle Shakespeare cut;
Wherein the graver had a strife
 With Nature, to out-do the life.
O, could he but have drawn his wit

Plate VII
Shakespeare — the Droeshout portrait, detail.

As well in brass, as he hath hit
His face, the print would then surpass
All that was ever writ in Brass.
But since he cannot, Reader, look
Not on his picture but his Book.

Heminge and Condell, who knew Shakespeare best, must have approved of the portrait or they surely would not have featured it on the title-page of their collection.

Commentators have not seen eye to eye concerning the Droeshout portrait, but they have disputed far more over the First Folio's dedicatory epistles. One of them, George Steevens, questioned the ability of Heminge and Condell to have written such 'literary' compositions. In the first place, the two epistles contain little or nothing that would entitle them to claim to be literary masterpieces. Secondly, certainly Heminge as business manager, and to a lesser extent Condell, who was also more interested in the organisation of the Company than in acting, were quite capable of expressing themselves with ease and lucidity. Steevens was undoubtedly stretching the evidence too far when he said that the epistles were the work of Ben Jonson. It is far more likely that Edward Blount, a man who could turn a neat phrase, helped the two editors with their epistles. He was, in any event, the most probable member of the consortium to have written so clearly and cogently. In any case, no matter who penned the prefatory material, Heminge and Condell cheerfully accepted full responsibility for the opinions put forward.

We now return to the plays themselves, setting down a passage from *King Lear* simply to give some idea of Heminge and Condell actually at work. In Act One, Scene One, the Quarto reads:

Regan: Sir, I am made of the selfe same mettall that my sister
is,

65

And prize me at her worth in my true heart,
I find she names my very deed of love, onely she came short,
That I professe myselfe an enemie to all other joyes,
Which the most precious square of sense possesses,
And find I am alone felicitate, in your deere Highnesse love.

The same speech in the Folio is rendered far more smoothly in these terms:

Regan: I am made of that selfe-mettle as my sister,
And prize me at her worth. In my true heart,
I finde she names my very deede of love:
Onely she comes too short, that I professe
My selfe an enemy to all other joyes,
Which the most precious square of sense professes,
And find I am alone felicitate
In your deere Highnesse love.

Continuing the exchange between Lear and Cordelia, the Quarto version is:

Lear: ...but now our joy,
Although the last, not least in our deere love,
What can you say to win a third, more opulent
Than your sisters?
Cord: Nothing, my lord.
Lear: How, nothing can come of nothing, speake againe.

Far more dramatic, especially in its repetition of the key word 'nothing', the Folio offers:

Lear: ...Now our Joy,
Although our last and least; to whose young love,
The Vines of France and Milke of Burgundie,
Strive to be interest. What can you say, to draw

A third, more opulent than your sisters? Speake.
Cord: Nothing, my lord.
Lear: Nothing?
Cord: Nothing.
Lear: Nothing will come of nothing, speake againe.

As a further illustration of how Heminge and Condell, through their persistence in seeking out the best available text, (i.e. the text that lay nearest to what the dramatist wanted to express), could transform indifferent material to blank verse of the highest order, the 1603 Quarto (admittedly a bad one) of *Hamlet* presents the most famous of all soliloquies in the following manner:

To be, or not to be, I there's the point.
To die, to sleepe, is that all? I all.
No, to sleepe, to dreame. I mary there it goes.
For in that dreame of death, when wee awake
And borne before an everlasting Judge,
From whence no passenger ever return'd,
The undiscovered country, at whose sight
The happy smile, and the accurs'd damn'd.
But for this, the joyfull hope of this,
Who'ld beare the scornes and flattery of the world,
Scorn'd by the right rich, the rich curs'd of the poore?
The widow being oppressed, the orphan wrong'd,
The taste of hunger, or a tirants raigne,
And thousand more calamities besides.
To grunt and sweate under this weary life
When that he may his full quietus make
With a bare bodkin, who would this indure,
But for a hope of something after death?
Which pusles the braine, and doth confound the sence
Which makes us rather beare these evilles we have
Than flie to others that we know not of.

I that, O this conscience makes cowards of us all.
Lady in thy orizons, be all my sinnes remembred.

Heminge and Condell, both of whom had acted alongside William Shakespeare in *Hamlet,* would never have dreamed of offering such a verbal gallimaufry to their readers. They would know exactly how the speech had been mutilated almost beyond recognition and how it had been assembled from the faulty recollections of some group of strolling players. No. doubt their own memory of the soliloquy would have been an improvement on the Quarto, but they would want to present authentic Shakespeare. After all, they had access to the official prompt-book and there they would find:

To be, or not to be — that is the question;
Whether 'tis nobler in the mind to suffer
The slings and arrows of outrageous fortune,
Or to take arms against a sea of troubles,
And by opposing end them? To die, to sleep —
No more; and by a sleep to say we end
The heart-ache, and the thousand natural shocks
That flesh is heir to. 'Tis a consummation
Devoutly to be wish'd. To die, to sleep;
To sleep, perchance to dream. Ay, there's the rub;
For in that sleep of death what dreams may come,
When we have shuffled off this mortal coil,
Must give us pause. There's the respect
That makes calamity of so long a life;
For who would bear the whips and scorns of time,
Th' oppressor's wrong, the proud man's contumely,
The pangs of despis'd love, the law's delay,
The insolence of office, and the spurns
That patient merit of th' unworthy takes,

When he himself might his quietus make
With a bare bodkin? . . .

But what need is there to complete Hamlet's best-known speech. The difference between the two versions is immediately apparent. George Ian Duthie in his critical study, *The 'Bad' Quarto of 'Hamlet'*, hits the nail on the head when he maintains that this particular Quarto stems from the complete Shakespearian version that lies behind the Second Quarto and the Folio. He has also discovered two distinct types of text in the 'Bad' Quarto. W. W. Greg sums up Duthie's argument admirably in the following words: 'The more prevalent type follows, or attempts to follow, the original fairly closely, being at its best an almost verbal reproduction, at its worst a string of phrases that makes little or no pretence to metre of even to consecutive sense . . . The other category consists of passages of usually correct but uniformly flat and evidently un-Shakespearian verse that render the general sense of the original, or at least occupy a corresponding position, but show little or no verbal similarity.'

Everyone is forced to agree that the Quarto soliloquy often slips into incomprehensibility. The Heminge and Condell version as presented in the First Folio is poetry at its very best. One can only marvel at such conscientious editorship.

VI

*. . .the abstracts and brief
chronicles of the time.*

ALSO included in the prefatory matter is a list of the
principal actors in the plays in the First Folio. Most of
them have already been mentioned, but a little
additional information about some of them will not be out of
place. After all, they were for many years the friends and
fellow actors of Shakespeare and our two gentlemen of
Aldermanbury. When the First Folio was published,
Shakespeare had been dead for seven years, but he is named
in the list at the head of the twenty-five King's Men. The
others in that honourable company are: Richard Burbage,
John Heminge, Augustine Phillips, William Kempe, Thomas
Pope, George Bryan, Henry Condell, William Sly, Richard
Cowley, John Lowin, Samuel Cross, Alexander Cooke,
Samuel Gilborne, Robert Armin, William Ostler, Nathan
Field, John Underwood, Nicholas Tooley, William
Ecclestone, Joseph Taylor, Robert Benfield, Robert Gough,
Richard Robinson, John Shank and John Rice.

Many of those, too, had died before the publication of the
plays in 1623, while two of them — Gough and Underwood

— died during the following year. Gough, who lived not far from the Globe, had served his stage apprenticeship under Thomas Pope. Underwood, who owned shares in three theatres, (Blackfriars, the Globe and the Curtain), was a wealthy man, living in Smithfield. Condell was his executor and Heminge was one of the overseers of his will.

If Shakespeare was the Company's dramatist, Richard Burbage was the group's outstanding actor. His father, who owned the Theatre and more or less controlled the Curtain, lived with his two sons, Cuthbert and Richard, in Holywell Street close to the two theatres. He had been an actor himself, so it is not really surprising that his sons were interested in the playhouse. In fact he made his stage debut early and by the time he was thirty he was known far and wide as the 'Roscius' of his age. In 1599 Richard and Cuthbert helped pull down the Shoreditch theatre and build the Globe for their summer productions.

The dismantling of the Theatre is vividly described by Giles Allen, the ground landlord. He says that the Burbages and their wrecking crew — their financial backer, their principal carpenter and about a dozen workmen — carried out the task on the night of December 28th, 1598. Burbage Senior had died the year before, but his widow was in attendance and no doubt spurred on their efforts. The demolition gang, according to Allen, did 'riotously assemble themselves together and then and there armed themselves with divers and many unlawful and offensive weapons, as namely, swords, daggers, bills, axes, and such like, and so armed did then repair unto the said Theatre. And then and there, armed as aforesaid, in very riotous, outrageous, and forcible manner, and contrary to the laws of your Highness's realm, attempted to pull down the said Theatre, whereupon divers of your subjects, servants and farmers, then going about in peaceable manner to procure them to desist from that their

unlawful enterprise, they, the said riotous persons aforesaid, notwithstanding procured then therein with great violence, not only then and there forcibly and riotously resisting your subjects, servants and farmers, but also then and there pulling, breaking, and throwing down the said Theatre in very outrageous, violent and riotous sort, to the great disturbance and terrifying not only of your subjects, said servants and farmers, but of divers others of your Majesty's loving subjects there near inhabiting'.

The Burbages and their helpers ferried the timbers across the Thames and built a splendid new playhouse which they called the Globe.

After reading how Richard Burbage played a part in this disturbance of the peace, we find it hard to believe that the poet John Davies of Hereford is writing about the same man in the lines that follow:

> *Players, I love ye and your quality*
> *As ye are men that pass time not abused;*
> *And some I love for painting, poesy,*
> *And say fell Fortune cannot be excused*
> *That hath for better uses you refused —*
> *Wit, courage, good shape, good parts, and all good*
> *(As long as all these goods are no worse used);*
> *And though the stage doth stain pure gentle blood,*
> *Yet generous ye are in mind and mood.*

The words 'And some I love for painting' clearly apply to Richard Burbage who was not only a great tragedian, but also a portrait painter of considerable merit.

Fifteen years later, of course, the Globe was burnt down, an event that was commemorated in the ballad already quoted from by virtue of the reference to 'old stuttering Heminges'. Other players running round rescuing various items from the

fire were Burbage, Robert Armin and Henry Condell, as the following verse testifies:

Out run the Knights, out run the Lords,
And there was great ado;
Some lost their hats, and some their swords —
Then out ran Burbage too:
The reprobates, though drunk on Monday,
Pray'd for the Fool [Robert Armin] and Henry Conday.

Another close friend of Heminge and Condell was William Kemp, small but strong, musical, and a natural wag who once, for a bet, danced all the way from London to Norwich, a performance that he himself celebrated in his *Kemps Nine Daies Wonder,* published in 1600.

The principal comedian in the Company had been Richard Tarlton, a man of lowly origin and little education, whose improvised witticisms, comic acting and recitations earned him a great deal of popularity. As a result of the dissipated life he led, he died in poverty in 1588. Kemp was the obvious choice to take over Tarlton's roles, especially those of clowns. Shakespeare must have introduced much of the real Kemp into such creations as Dromio, Grumio, Launce, Gobbo, Costard and Dogberry. In the second part of *Henry VI* York's description of Jack Cade fits Kemp to perfection:

... I have seen
Him caper upright like a wild Morisco,
Shaking the bloody darts as he his bells,
Full often like a shag-hair'd crafty kerne.

Equally appropriate are the lines in part two of *Henry IV* where Falstaff is describing Shallow, (played by Kemp and an obvious piece of type-casting). Falstaff says, 'I do remember him like a man made after supper of a cheese-paring; when a was naked he was for all the world like a forked radish, with a

head fantastically carved upon it with a knife . . . If I were sawed into quantities, I should make four dozen of such bearded hermits' staves as Master Shallow'.

Kemp's farewell to the stage is typical of that odd little man. After returning from his celebrated jig from London to Norwich, he felt that he had 'danced himself out of the World' (the Globe?). Addressing ballad-makers who had ridiculed him, he said, 'I am shortly, God willing, to set forward as merrily as I may, whither I myself know not. Wherefore employ not your little wits in certifying the world that I am gone to Rome, Jerusalem, Venice, or any other place . . .'

Kemp died in what to-day would be called 'distressed circumstances' borrowing small amounts to keep him going until his death towards the end of 1603. It was plague time, a possible explanation for the brief entry in the church register:

1603 November 2nd William Kemp, a man.

The actor who took over as low comedian from William Kemp in Shakespeare's Company was Robert Armin from King's Lynn. Once a goldsmith, he joined Lord Chandos's Players and in 1599, probably invited to do so by Shakespeare, he joined the dramatist's Company. Following on after Kemp as Dogberry, he must have proved a satisfactory substitute for he stayed with Shakespeare's group until he died. He was a clown all right, but on an intellectual level. He could have played, for instance, Touchstone, Trinculo, Feste, and the very different kind of fool we have in *King Lear*. It was as the Clown in *All's Well That Ends Well,* that he acted alongside Burbage as Bertram, Heminge as Lafeu, and Cowley as the Cockscomb, and with Ecclestone and Gilborne (or Gough) as 'Brother Lords'. In Augustine Phillip's will he was left twenty shillings in gold. A tribute to his ability as an actor is voiced by John Davies of Hereford who writes in his *The Scourge of Folly*:

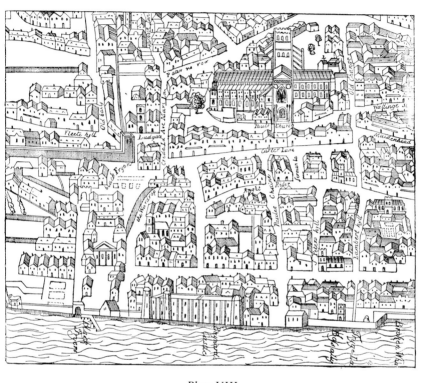

Plate VIII
St. Paul's and Blackfriars, 1563
(From Aggas's Plan)

Armin, what shall I say to thee but this,
Thou art a fool and knave? Fie, I miss
And wrong thee much, since thou indeed art neither,
Although in show thou playest both together.
We all (that's Kings and all) but players are
Upon this earthly stage; and should have care
To play our parts so properly that we
May at the end gain an applaudite.

Also close to Heminge, Condell and Shakespeare was Augustine Phillips who died at Mortlake in 1607. He made his will early in May and declared that he commended his soul into the hands of Almighty God, 'my Maker and Saviour and Redeemer, in whom and by the merits of the Second Person, Jesus Christ, I trust and believe assuredly to be saved, and to have clear remission and forgiveness of my sins; and I commit my body to be buried in the chancel of the parish-church'. To Shakespeare he left 'a thirty shilling piece in gold; to my fellow, Henry Condell, one other thirty shilling piece in gold', and to some of his other 'fellows' varying amounts, always in gold.

Mention is made of Phillips (and other actors) in Heywood's *An Apology for Actors,* in which the author vigorously defends his profession in the following terms:

I must needs remember Tarleton ... Gabriel Spenser, Singer, Pope, Phillips, Sly — all the right I can do them is but this, that though they be dead, their deserts yet live in the remembrance of many ... I could wish that such as are condemned for their licentiousness, might by a general consent be quite excluded our society; for as we are men that stand in the broad eye of the world, so should our manners, gestures and behaviours savour of such government and modesty, to deserve the good thoughts and reports of all

77

men, and to abide the sharpest censures even of those that are the greatest opposites to the quality.

Of the 'Principall Actors' in the plays, we have a special regard for Augustine Phillips. For more than ten years he had worked with Shakespeare. He was one of the Company's original 'sharers'. He had acted in Shakespeare's plays and had actually appeared in pieces alongside the dramatist himself. He and his family had lived near the Bankside theatre district in Southwark, but just before his death he had moved to Mortlake.

Phillips' widow, Anne, contracted an unfortunate marriage with the rogue John Witter already mentioned, the man who sued Heminge and Condell for Phillips' share of the actors' part of the Globe. By marrying again, Anne Phillips had forfeited her interest in Augustine's estate, but Heminge had leased the Witters a share for eighteen years. When Witter had fallen behind in his ground rent payments, Heminge had cancelled the lease. This did not deter Witter from bringing an action against Heminge and Condell, hoping to recover his share. As might have been expected, the Witter suit was dismissed.

One of the founder members of the Chamberlain's Company was Thomas Pope. In 1586, when he was one of Leicester's Men, (together with George Bryan, Kemp, his apprentice and others), Pope toured in Denmark. It is an interesting thought that Shakespeare's knowledge of Elsinore and the Danes was probably picked up in conversation with his three 'fellows'.

Pope and Phillips were very close and might have been kinsmen. Both lived in Southwark, were comfortably off, and like Bryan and Heminge, were 'Masters' in their profession.

In the presentation of *Romeo and Juliet* at the Theatre, if Burbage played Romeo, Shakespeare the Friar, Heminge Capulet, and Kemp Peter, it is quite likely that Pope took the

Plate IX
William Sly, one of the King's Men.

part of the Nurse, while his apprentice, Robert Gough, was Juliet. Another part that might have been written for Pope was that of Jaques in *As You Like It*. (The 'tormenting laughter' and 'goggle eye', ascribed to him by Ben Jonson, would not have been out of place in the melancholy foreigner).

Among the members of the Lord Chamberlain's Company especially liked by Heminge and Condell was Thomas Pope. It was in 1594 that Lord Strange's Company passed over to the patronage of Lord Hunsdon, and it was at that time that Shakespeare first became involved with the Lord Chamberlain's Men, both as an actor and as an author. Thomas Pope was one of their principal actors.

In a revolutionary approach to theatre ownership, a syndicate was formed to run the Globe by the very men who built the new theatre. The Burbage brothers held a half-interest; the other half-share was leased by the owner, Nicholas Brend, to Shakespeare, Heminge, Phillips, Kemp and Thomas Pope. The new proprietors of the Globe were henceforth known as 'house-keepers'. When Kemp withdrew from the organisation, each of the other four players was responsible for one-eighth of the theatre shares.

As for Pope's physical appearance, Professor Baldwin sees him as a Falstaffian kind of comic, an image supported by Samuel Rowlands, writer of satirical tracts in prose and verse round about the turn of the 16th/17th century, who saw Pope in the role of an ill-mannered clown. On the other hand, in *Spring, 1600,* Emlyn Williams presents Pope as a gentle feline type who might well have played Gertrude in *Hamlet.*

Of the other actors we know that Alexander Cooke was particularly friendly with Shakespeare and might well have started his theatrical career as an apprentice to Heminge. Richard Cowley was a low comedian who played, among other suitable roles, Verges in *Much Ado About Nothing.*

Samuel Crosse was at his best in comic female roles and most probably was given parts such as Maria in *Twelfth Night* and Mistress Quickly in *The Merry Wives of Windsor*. Nathan Field, originally a boy actor at Blackfriars Theatre, filled the vacancy left by Shakespeare's death. Samuel Gilborne started off as an apprentice actor to Augustine Phillips who held him in such esteem that in his will he left him a bass viol. A big man in every sense was John Lowin who had joined the King's Men in 1603. Like Heminge and Condell, he displayed an interest in the business side of theatre management. Physically he was a large man who would have been entirely at home in the part of Falstaff.

Several of the players appeared in a curiously composite performance entitled *Four Plays in One,* including Richard Cowley as the Lieutenant of the Tower, Henry Condell and William Sly as Ferrex and Porrex, Nicholas Tooley as 'a Lady', Robert Gough as Aspatria, Cooke as Progne, Gilborne as Mercury, Shakespeare as King Henry, Heminge as Lydgate the Poet, Burbage as Gorboduc, Bryan as Damasus, Augustine Phillips as Sardanapalus, Pope as Arbactus, and John Sinkler as 'a Keeper'.

It cannot be denied that this body of players outshone all the other theatrical companies of their day.

It is ironical that, thanks to the labours of Heminge and Condell, the fame of William Shakespeare has spread throughout the world. Furthermore, even though he died as long ago as 1619, Richard Burbage too, because he had the good fortune to play the superb roles Shakespeare created for him, is affectionately remembered, and not only by Shakespearian scholars. Yet if the names of Heminge and Condell mean anything at all to-day, (and perhaps they do to a handful of critics, commentators and drama students), it is largely owing to the fact that generations of men of letters have misunderstood their motives, accusing them of

Plate X
Hall's painting of the bust of Shakespeare.

self-interest and profiteering. Their disparagers deny that Heminge and Condell were the 'pious fellows' described by Leonard Digges and maintain that they edited the plays solely to enhance their own reputations.

The truth is that Heminge and Condell had known and worked with Shakespeare for about thirty years and looked upon him as their very close friend. When Burbage died in 1619, Heminge and Condell were the only surviviors of the King's Men sufficiently qualified to comb through the many varied Shakespearian texts and pick out the best for publication. It was a tremendous responsibility, for there was no one else to ensure that their leading dramatist's works would receive adequate recognition and that they would be presented as nearly as possible in the form in which Shakespeare conceived them. Never before had editorship demanded such meticulous attention to detail. Never before had editors been called upon to exercise so much authority. The two gentlemen from Aldermanbury had to sift carefully through a mass of material, rejecting all doubtful texts and retaining only what they believed to be authentic Shakespeare.

Although they were share-holders in both the Globe and Blackfriars, they need not necessarily have had any proprietary rights in the plays, which would most likely have been considered as falling under the ownership of the Company. On the other hand, as two of the King's Men's principal actors and as personal friends of the playwright himself, they must have had ready access to all the manuscripts and prompt-books, 'foul' and 'fair' papers, quartos and other documents collected over the years by the Company. They were clearly familiar with both good and bad versions of the plays. In their epistle to 'the great Variety of Readers' they refer to the public being cheated with a number of stolen or pirated texts that had been altered and

distorted by unauthorised hacks and published without proper authority. Such travesties, they continued 'are now offer'd to your view, cur'd, and perfect of their limbes; and all the rest absolute in their numbers, as he conceived them.'

It was largely a misunderstanding of the two prefatory epistles that led to the undeserved condemnation of Heminge and Condell. If the addresses are accepted as sincere expressions of the editors' sentiments and beliefs, they present no problems. The best approach is to dismiss at the outset any suggestion that somebody else, (Ben Jonson, for instance), wrote the letters, or that Heminge and Condell were assisted by Edward Blount, the one member of the publishing syndicate who had already penned similar dedications. Surely the real point is that the editors were prepared to put their signatures to the epistles and consequently take full responsibility for their contents.

Taking another look at the plays themselves, the first question we ask ourselves is — what about copyright?

The plain fact is that copyright as we understand it to-day, (that is to say, the legal protection of an author's interests), simply did not exist. In 1581 plays had to be submitted to the Master of the Revels whose job it was to vet them for political subversion and religious controversy. Twenty-six years later, plays could not be printed without the same official's seal of approval. Dramatists and actors alike were not in favour of plays being printed for sale to the general public. They believed that publication would inevitably lead to a dropping off in theatre attendance and a consequent diminution of 'box office' receipts.

Apart from the University presses of Oxford and Cambridge, the Stationers' Company held a monopoly for printing books in England. Booksellers and printers registered their work, paying the Company's fees, so in a sense there was a *kind* of copyright. The trouble was that the

system did not work satisfactorily. Plays were sometimes printed without the registration fee being paid; there were also cases of pirated plays being registered.

In Shakespeare's case, of course, whenever he wrote a play, the procedure was straightforward enough. It became the property of the Chamberlain's Men, (subsequently the King's Men). Playwrights were not particularly well remunerated in those days, but we must remember that as early as 1594 Shakespeare was much more than a small-time actor, for by then he had become a part-owner of the Company, sharing in the receipts at regular performances and being paid handsomely for Court appearances. Five years later he was also a 'house-keeper' at the Globe.

If, as F.E. Halliday informs us, his annual income amounted to two hundred pounds or thereabouts, Shakespeare would have been earning in to-day's values the equivalent of £5000. The plague years were much less lucrative, for the Company was obliged to leave the capital and tour the not so wealthy provinces.

Contemporary records all suggest that Shakespeare worked at a tremendous speed. *The Merry Wives of Windsor*, for example, was probably written in about a fortnight, but that was by way of being a royal request. His inspiration seemed to have emerged in great bursts of energy, and after creating each masterpiece, he showed little or no interest in the finished product other than attending to its successful production on the stage. There would be a period of calm and then he would suddenly be off again on some new project. Perhaps Jonson had him in mind when he described someone he knew in the following terms:

Ease and relaxation are profitable to all studies. The mind is like a bow, the stronger by being unbent. But the temper in spirits is all, when to command a man's wit, when to favour it. I have known a man vehement on both sides, that knew no

mean either to intermit his studies or call upon them again. When he hath set himself to writing, he would join night to day; press upon himself without release, not minding it till he fainted: and when he left off, resolve himself into all sports and looseness again; that it was almost a despair to draw him to his book: but once got to it, he grew stronger and more earnest by the ease.

It is not surprising that a dramatist with Shakespeare's temperament had little time to spare for the needs of posterity. The news that Ben Jonson was publishing his *Works,* he probably greeted with an appreciative chuckle. Although the First Folio did not appear until seven years after his death, there is no reason why, before he retired to Stratford, he should not have discussed the possibilities of an 'omnibus' volume with his good friends Heminge and Condell. Burbage, too, might well have been consulted. Shakespeare might even have given the venture his blessing, but he was also capable of asking his 'fellows' not to bother *him* about the matter.

Once the scheme was under way, Heminge and Condell were clearly out on their own. When they said, in their address to the two Earls, that their province was 'onely to gather his works', they meant precisely that. As far as they knew, there were thirty-six plays to be collected and edited. The five stationers who were backing the undertaking had rights to half-a-dozen of them. Sixteen had been registered in 1623. The rights of the remaining twenty had already been entered. Deducting the six held by the syndicate, we see that permission to print fourteen had to be obtained. A copyholder named Law had entered *Richard II, Richard III* and the first part of *Henry IV,* Thomas Pavier had the rights of a further three plays, and different stationers owned the other eight. Heminge and Condell had to approach no fewer than ten stationers before they could go ahead with their task. If

the stationers had died in the meantime, the two editors were obliged to seek the sanction of their executors. If the rights had changed hands, they had to apply to the new owners.

Sometimes there were complications. Smethwick, for instance, one of the publishing team, held the rights of an old play, *The Taming of A Shrew*. He was thus allowed to bring out *The Taming of The Shrew*, Shakespeare's amended version, without applying for a new entrance. In the same way, after the 1591 printing of *The Troublesome Raigne of John King of England*, Shakespeare's later version, simply called *King John*, emerged without being officially entered. Also among other plays presenting Heminge and Condell with copyright difficulties were *Henry V*, *King Lear* (entered to two different persons on the same day!), *Troilus and Cressida* (long considered to be a tragedy and never acted, whereas it is a comedy and was acted at Court and later at the Globe or Blackfriars), *Hamlet* with its wide variety of independent texts), and *Antony and Cleopatra* (entered by Edward Blount in 1608, but not printed until it was re-registered and printed in the First Folio in 1623).

VII

The play's the thing.

Shakespeare

ONCE THE PLAYS were assembled and the rights of publication obtained, Heminge and Condell had to start thinking about the way in which their 'omnibus' volume should be presented. The plays obviously fitted into three distinct groups — comedies, histories and tragedies — and as far as the histories were concerned, their order in the Catalogue was self-determined. Logically they had to appear in chronological sequence.

No doubt the editors had their reasons for listing the fourteen comedies first, the eleven tragedies third, with the ten history plays in the middle. (The temporary omission of the thirty-sixth play, *Troilus and Cressida*, has already been explained. *Pericles* was admitted later, in the Third Folio of 1664.) Heminge and Condell probably arranged their wares so that the most attractive items, the comedies, were the ones most prominently displayed. They themselves, however, were very likely particularly interested in the neat package of history plays and perhaps completed that section first.

Apart from these obvious divisions and the more or less compulsory time sequence for the histories, there is little

Plate XI
Shakespeare's monument in Holy Trinity Church, Stratford-upon-Avon.

evidence of any revolutionary editorial policy. The plays certainly do not appear in the order in which they were written. The comedy section, for instance, is headed by *The Tempest*, which was almost the last play Shakespeare wrote. An examination of the rest of the comedies, bearing in mind the dates of composition, suggests at first that they were listed more or less haphazardly. Could it be that Heminge and Condell, collecting their material from a dozen different sources, simply dealt with the plays as they came to hand? They may even have been tempted to let *The Tempest* stand as the *last* play in the First Folio, so that the reader could have been left with what must have been an echo of Shakespeare's farewell to the theatre:

Our revels now are ended. These our actors,
As I foretold you, were all spirits, and
Are melted into air, into thin air;
And, like the baseless fabric of this vision,
The cloud-capp'd towers, the gorgeous palaces,
The solemn temples, the great globe itself,
Yea, all which it inherit, shall dissolve,
And, like this insubstantial pageant faded,
Leave not a rack behind. We are such stuff
As dreams are made on; and our little life
Is rounded with a sleep.

There is, however, much to support Professor Pollard's contention that, apart from the histories, 'so far as the history and accidents of the press would allow, the editors placed unprinted plays in all the important positions, and hid away those already printed in the middle of them.' He also maintained that there were two types of Tragedy — Classical and Post-Classical. It would certainly appear that Pollard was right when he said that the printed plays fall into groups.

To begin with the comedies, there were the reprinted quartos. Then there were the written prompt-books. Thirdly there were what Sir Sidney Lee refers to as 'the less complete and less authentic transcripts in private hands', assembled texts, i.e. those made up of the separate actors' scripts fitted together in the manner of a jigsaw puzzle into one neat version. Three of these assembled texts — *The Two Gentlemen of Verona, The Merry Wives of Windsor* and *Measure for Measure* — lie together, second, third and fourth in the Folio. The fifth play, *The Comedy of Errors,* although most likely based on 'foul' papers, has many of the characteristics of an assembled text.

The next four comedies, *Much Ado About Nothing, Love's Labour's Lost, A Midsummer Night's Dream* and *The Merchant of Venice* can also be grouped together in so far as they were all reprinted from quartos.

Then we get *As You Like It, The Taming of the Shrew, All's Well that Ends Well* and *Twelfth Night,* in that order, forming a batch because none of them had been published before and the Folio version of each was based on a written prompt-book.

Thus we are left with *The Tempest* and *The Winter's Tale,* both written towards the end of Shakespeare's career as a dramatist. If, as seems likely, they were the last two comedies the editors dealt with, their easiest course was to list them first and last, positions they could occupy without disturbing the sequence of the other plays.

The Histories do not fall into batches, but the Tragedies can be grouped into reprints from the Quartos, (*Titus Andronicus, Romeo and Juliet, Troilus and Cressida*); unpublished plays in manuscripts, (*Timon of Athens, Julius Caesar, Macbeth*); manuscripts (prompt-books?) of former Quarto versions, (*Hamlet, King Lear, Othello*); and a couple of prompt-books, (*Antony and Cleopatra* and *Cymbeline*)

94

How *Troilus and Cressida* was accidentally placed among the tragedies, removed and overlooked, and finally set between the Histories and Comedies, has already been explained.

The views of Nicholas Rowe, dramatist, poet and Shakespearian editor, are also relevant and worth quoting. In his 1709 edition of Shakespeare's plays, he says:

> *His Plays are properly to be distinguish'd only into Comedies and Tragedies. Those which are called Histories, and even some of his Comedies, are really Tragedies, with a run or mixture of Comedy amongst 'em. That way of Trage-Comedy was the common Mistake of that Age, and is indeed become so agreeable to the English Taste, that tho' the severer critiques among us cannot bear it, yet the generality of our Audiences seem better pleas'd with it than with an exact Tragedy. 'The Merry Wives of Windsor', 'The Comedy of Errors', and 'The Taming of the Shrew', are all pure comedy; the rest, however they are call'd, have something of both kinds.*

Under the title 'Master William Shakespeare's Comedies, Histories and Tragedies', the famous First Folio emerged from the press in 1623. Containing about nine hundred pages, the volume sold at one pound — good value for money in those days when an old Quarto edition cost no more than sixpence. As for the number of copies printed, there is very little agreement among the commentators, some putting the figure as low as 250, other making it as high as a thousand. A first print of a thousand would certainly have made it a viable commercial proposition.

Nine years were to elapse before the publication of the Second Folio (1632), which is more or less a reproduction of its predecessor. After a long gap of thirty-one years the Third Folio appeared, much like the two previous editions except for the inclusion of *Pericles*. Heminge and Condell could no longer object to it as non-Shakespearian as both were dead.

Other plays introduced into the Third Folio were *The London Prodigal, The History of Thomas, Lord Cromwell, Sir John Oldcastle, The Puritan Widow, A Yorkshire Tragedy, The Tragedy of Locrine.* The Fourth Folio followed on twenty-one years later, very little different from the Third. The long intervals between folios suggest that sales, although not encouraging, were at least there. Shakespeare, thanks to that timely First Folio was remembered and was being read.

A further twenty-four years passed by before a new edition of Shakespeare was printed. Put together by Nicholas Rowe, illustrated, attractively presented in six octavo volumes, it was the first collection to include a life of the author. Rowe actually goes as far as giving a personal description of Shakespeare, although he produces nothing by way of corroboration. He says:

> *Besides the advantages of his Wit, he was in himself a good-natur'd Man, of great sweetness in his Manners, and a most agreeable Companion; so that it is no wonder if with so many good qualities he made himself acquainted with the best Conversations of those Times ... His exceeding Candor and good Nature must certainly have inclin'd all the gentler Part of the World to love him, as the power of his Wit oblig'd the Men of the most delicate Knowledge and polite Learning to admire him.*

Rowe's volume had much to commend it. It was a great pity, however, that the compiler chose to base his texts on the Fourth Folio.

After Rowe's collection, editions of Shakespeare's works came thick and fast — Alexander Pope (1725), Lewis Theobald (1734), Thomas Hanmer (1744), William Warburton (1747), Samuel Johnson (1765), Edward Capell (1768), George Steevens (1773), Edmond Malone (1790), John Payne Collier (1824-44), James Halliwell-Phillips

Plate XII
Richard Burbage, the Company's principal actor.

(1853-65), Alexander Dyce (1857), William Aldis Wright (1863-9), and in the present century, G. L. Kittredge (1936), Peter Alexander (1952), C. J. Sisson (1954), John Munro (1958) and others have edited Shakespeare's plays/works. Our two gentlemen of Aldermanbury certainly started something . . .

Of the many editions of Shakespeare's plays, the one that inevitably takes pride of place is the 1623 First Folio. Without it, English literature would have been the poorer by eighteen dramatic masterpieces, all of which were printed for the first time in the Heminge and Condell collection. We should have gone without:

Julius Caesar
As You Like It
Twelfth Night
All's Well that Ends Well.
Measure for Measure.
Macbeth.
Antony and Cleopatra.
Coriolanus.
Henry VIII.
Henry VI Part One
Two Gentlemen of Verona
Comedy of Errors
The Taming of the Shrew
King John
Timon of Athens
Cymbeline.
The Winter's Tale
The Tempest

In short we should have been deprived of fifty per cent of

the plays of a man who seemed 'to have known the world by intuition'. Without the dedication and conscientiousness of Heminge and Condell, we should never have been acquainted with such fascinating characters as Jaques, Malvolio, the Porter in *Macbeth*, Feste, Touchstone, Caliban, Autolycus, Sir Toby Belch, Sir Andrew Aguecheek and a host of others. Benham's *Book of Quotations* would have had well over six hundred fewer entries, including such precious gems as:

Between the acting of a dreadful thing
And the first motion, all the interim is
Like a phantasma, or a hideous dream.
                                        Julius Caesar

Sweet are the uses of adversity;
Which, like the toad, ugly and venomous,
Wears yet a precious jewel in his head:
And this our life, exempt from public haunts,
Finds tongues in trees, books in the running brooks,
Sermons in stones, and good in everything.
                                        As You Like It

Dost thou think, because thou art virtuous, there
shall be no more cakes and ale?
                                        Twelfth Night

'Let me not live,' quoth he,
'After my flame lacks oil, to be the snuff
Of younger spirits.'
                                        All's Well that Ends Well

    But man, proud man!
Drest in a little brief authority, —
Most ignorant of what he's most assured,
His glassy essence, — like an angry ape,
Plays such fantastic tricks before high heaven,
As make the angels weep.
                                        Measure for Measure

100

Methought I heard a voice cry, 'Sleep no more!
Macbeth does murder sleep,' — the innocent sleep;
Sleep that knits up the ravelled sleave of care,
The death of each day's life, sore labour's bath,
Balm of hurt minds, great Nature's second course,
Chief nourisher in life's feast.

Macbeth

We can never pay sufficient homage to the industrious editors of the 1623 First Folio. Over three and a half centuries have passed by since the publication of their 'omnibus' volume and throughout all those years they have rarely received their due acclaim. The two men who literally gave us Shakespeare have been conveniently pushed into the background and forgotten. In *The Oxford Companion to English Literature,* for instance, Heminge does not even warrant an individual mention. The entry runs:

Heming or Heminges, John (d. 1630) and Condell, Henry (d. 1627), fellow actors of Shakespeare, who jointly edited the first folio of his plays (1623). Heming is said to have been the first actor of Falstaff.

While Condell is even more scurvily treated. He is disposed of in one laconic line:

Condell, Henry, see Heming.

Moreover, in the 1938 edition of Chamber's *Biographical Dictionary,* both are completely ignored.

It may well be that Heminge and Condell were occasionally in error. For instance, such eminent Shakespearian scholars as A. W. Pollard, W. W. Greg, Sir Edward Maunde Thompson, J. Dover Wilson and R. W. Chambers argue forcibly that at least *part* of *The Booke of Sir Thomas More* was written by Shakespeare, although Heminge and Condell completely excluded it from the First Folio. In the same way

101

our two editors rejected *Pericles* as non-Shakespearian and yet it was included in the Third Folio of 1664 and is now in the Stratford repertoire.

In both cases their judgments may have been at fault, but as our main concern is to ensure some measure of recognition and appreciation for the two gentlemen of Aldermanbury, it is easy to overlook such minor lapses among so many outstanding achievements. If they did not always hit the mark, we can readily forgive them for they were doing their best.

We owe much to the painstaking work of editors and scholars, and there is still scope for discovery, but without Heminge and Condell a great deal would have been lost for ever.

Perhaps in their case it would be more appropriate to let their friend Shakespeare have the last word —

For never anything can be amiss
When simpleness and duty tender it.

Plate XIII
Above; Conjectural drawing of the Church of St. Mary Aldermanbury, City of London. Below; as rebuilt by Sir Christopher Wren in 1677 after the Great Fire.

Plate XIV
The bomb-ruined remains of the Church of St. Mary-the-Virgin, Aldermanbury, as it stood in London, England, before being dismantled, cleaned, marked and shipped to Westminster College for restoration as the Winston Churchill Memorial & Library of the United States.

Plate XV
Church of St. Mary Aldermanbury rebuilt at Westminster College, Fulton, Missouri.

Notes

1. All manner of interesting information concerning Shakespeare, Heminge and Condell may be gleaned from *The Stationers' Register,* various wills, legal documents (including law-suits), contemporary allusions, diaries, Register of Stratford Parish Church, histories of players' companies, property deeds, Court payments for play productions, formal Patents, indentures, letters, miscellaneous papers and internal evidence in the actual plays.

2. These London companies elected John Heminge to negotiate as their agent with the Master of the Revels in 1618, the year before Burbage died.

3. There were quarto versions of individual plays, sometimes several quartos of the same play, (as mentioned on page 49). Heminge and Condell, realising that there were too many (36) plays to present in a quarto edition, turned to the only solution — the heavy expense of printing them in folio.

Selected Bibliography

Alexander, Peter, *Shakespeare's Life and Art,* Nisbet, 1939.
Bliss, William, *The Real Shakespeare,* London, 1947.
Brown, Ivor, *Shakespeare,* London, 1949.
Chambers, E.K., *The Elizabethan Stage,* 4 vols., Oxford, 1923.
Chambers, E.K., *William Shakespeare: A Study of Facts and Problems,* O.U.P., 1930.
Crompton Rhodes, R., *Shakespeare's First Folio,* Oxford, 1923.
Fripp, Edgar I., *Shakespeare, Man & Artist,* 2 vols., O.U.P., 1938.
Granville-Barker, H. & Harrison, G.B., (Eds.) *A Companion to Shakespeare Studies,* C.U.P.., 1946.
Greg, W.W., *The Editorial Problem in Shakespeare,* Oxford, 1954.
Greg, W.W., *The Shakespeare First Folio,* Oxford, 1955.
Lloyd Evans, G. & B., *Everyman's Companion to Shakespeare,* Dent, 1978.
Rowse, A.L., *William Shakespeare, A Biography,* London, 1963.
Schoenbaum, S., *Shakespeare's Lives,* O.U.P., 1970.
Schoenbaum, S., *William Shakespeare: A Compact Documentary Life,* O.U.P., 1977.
Speaight, R., *Shakespeare,* Dent, 1977.
Walker, C.C., *John Heminge & Henry Condell,* privately printed.
Wilson, J. Dover, *Essential Shakespeare: A Biographical Adventure,* C.U.P., 1932.

The author acknowledges his considerable debt to many scholars in addition to those listed above. As this book is not primarily about Shakespeare but about the men who gave us Shakespeare, a mass of references to the work of other Shakespearian specialists would not be appropriate. Readers who wish to follow up matters of Shakespearian scholarship which are referred to in the text may usefully start with the titles here given.